948 229

6⁹⁵ɯ

Exile
in the
Fatherland

Martin Niemöller's
Letters from Moabit Prison

Translated by
Ernst Kaemke, Kathy Elias, and Jacklyn Wilferd

Edited by
Hubert G. Locke

WILLIAM B. EERDMANS PUBLISHING COMPANY
GRAND RAPIDS, MICHIGAN

Translated from *Martin Niemöller: Briefe aus der Gefangenschaft Moabit*,
ed. Wilhelm Niemöller
Copyright © 1975 by Verlag Otto Lembeck, Frankfurt

Published in cooperation with the William O. Douglas Institute

Library of Congress Cataloging in Publication Data

Niemöller, Martin, 1892–
Exile in the Fatherland.

Translation of: Briefe aus der Gefangenschaft Moabit.
1. Niemöller, Martin, 1892–   —Correspondence.
I. Locke, Hubert G. II. Title.
BX8080.N48A4 1986   284.1'092'4 [B]   86-491

ISBN 0-8028-3610-0

CONTENTS

FOREWORD

The death of Martin Niemöller in the spring of 1984 removed from the international scene one of the most striking personalities in twentieth-century Christianity. A leader in the church struggle with Nazism, he became known as "Pastor Niemöller" to a whole generation of Christian leaders outside Germany. He was already well known in his native land as a war hero in World War I and as a popular preacher in one of the most prestigious pulpits in Germany, Berlin-Dahlem. From July 1937 until he was liberated at the end of the war, Martin Niemöller was held in prison and concentration camp, for most of that time as the "personal prisoner" of Adolf Hitler. Niemöller later attributed his survival to the fact that intercessory services were held on his behalf throughout the Christian world and that the Nazis were never able to act in total disregard of mobilized religious opinion.

In any case Martin Niemöller did survive to become one of the most prominent postwar Christian leaders—as president of the protestant synod of Hesse, as a preacher and teacher in such a movement as the Deutscher Evangelischer Kirchentag (the largest laymen's movement in the world), as a president of the World Council of Churches, and as a spokesman on behalf of civil rights and peace. The adult education center (Evangelische Akademie) of Hesse now bears his name.

Shortly after World War II ended, Niemöller participated in the meeting which framed the Stuttgart Declaration of Guilt (October 19, 1945). He traveled through the United States and concluded many of his addresses with the now famous statement:

First they came for the socialists, and I did not speak out—
  because I was not a socialist.
Then they came for the trade unionists, and I did not speak
    out—
  because I was not a trade unionist.
Then they came for the Jews, and I did not speak out—
  because I was not a Jew.
Then they came for me—and there was no one left to speak
  for me.

If Karl Barth was the most important theologian of the church resistance to Nazism, Martin Niemöller was until his imprisonment its primary strategist. He founded the Pastors' Emergency League and was a key figure in the Confessing church (Bekennende Kirche) which emerged from the Barmen synod of May 29–31, 1934. By the time he was arrested and imprisoned, first in Moabit and later in Sachsenhausen and Dachau, where he was held without trial or charge on direct order of the Führer, the basic lines of the Christian resistance were set: the Nazi regime was resisted for invading the church's area of competence and for idolatry—not for breaking the law or for its brutal breach of the rights of human beings. Niemöller, who was at the time a religious and political conservative, was in any case opposed to political resistance.

After the war, Martin Niemöller confessed publicly not only his failure to assess properly the demonic nature of Nazism but also his failure—which he attributed to his theological training in Lutheranism—to understand that there come times when Christians have not only the right but the duty to resist evil regimes. He became in his later years a Christian pacifist and a leader in the religious resistance to armaments, especially nuclear weapons.

Niemöller's admission of earlier "failures," like his participation in the Stuttgart Declaration, was typical of the man. Enormously gifted as a preacher and leader, he lived by faith—and was able to stand for the right at all risk and to admit error in all humility.

I shall never forget a Dutch theological student whom I met when traveling to the first World Christian Youth conference in Amsterdam in August 1939. This student talked to me passionately about the church struggle and the demonic nature of Nazism and its Führer, and he gave me a book of Niemöller's sermons which I still treasure: *Dennoch getrost.* When I remarked that I had heard nothing recently of Martin Niemöller, an unusual thing because of the churches' concern, he exploded, "Then they've killed him!" In his tone of voice and in his attachment, in his identification with Niemöller and the other German brethren who were resisting the Nazis, I had a sudden realization that nothing the Nazis could do would defeat what Martin Niemöller then represented. In life or in death, his message would triumph over the princes and powers of this world's darkness.

Martin Niemöller and his brother Wilhelm took an active interest in the development of the Annual Scholars Conference on the Holocaust and the Church Struggle (founded in 1970, with Wilhelm Niemöller one of the major lecturers). Both of them had promised to attend the Annual Scholars Conference which celebrated the fiftieth anniversary of the Barmen Declaration in Seattle (April 1984) if health permitted, but they died within a few weeks of each other, advanced in years. (Martin Niemöller was ninety-two.) We can be grateful to Hubert Locke for his efforts in making this book of Martin Niemöller's Christian thought available to the world of the churches and the campuses.

Temple University   FRANKLIN H. LITTELL
Philadelphia

ACKNOWLEDGMENTS

In addition to the devoted work of the three translators who spent countless hours rendering the German text into an appropriate English style, grateful appreciation is expressed to Linda K. Christian-Locke for her diligent efforts in typing, often from scraps of paper and almost indecipherable marginal notes, the English translation of the text. The Introduction was typed by Mrs. Thelma Brown, whose passion for the period of the German church struggle was greatly enhanced by her service as secretary to the International Symposium of Scholars and Church Leaders, held in 1984 to commemorate the fiftieth anniversary of the Barmen synod and its declaration. Finally, the German texts of these letters were first transmitted to me by Martin Niemöller's younger brother, Wilhelm, through my one-time secretary and dear friend, Christine Lovio-George. Ms. Lovio-George was secretary to the first International Scholars Conference on the Church Struggle and the Holocaust in 1970, which Pastor Wilhelm Niemöller attended and addressed. He and Ms. Lovio-George continued a lively correspondence for many years thereafter; it is with much warmth and affection that I acknowledge her initial efforts which led to the preparation of the English text.

The William O. Douglas Institute   HUBERT G. LOCKE
Seattle

Exile in the Fatherland

INTRODUCTION

This volume of letters, written to his family, colleagues, parishioners, and friends by a man who, only a few years before they were penned, was a Lutheran pastor relatively unknown outside Germany and serving his first parish in a suburb of Berlin, would have little significance for others than those to whom they were sent were it not for the extraordinary circumstances which brought them about. They were written over a period of eight months by a man who was a political prisoner—Adolf Hitler's personal prisoner—jailed for having organized the first serious public opposition to Hitler's leadership as chancellor of the German Third Reich. That opposition earned for the author of these letters Hitler's undying enmity. Arrested by the gestapo on July 1, 1937, he was held for eight months at the prison in Moabit, subsequently placed— on Hitler's direct orders—in solitary confinement in the concentration camp at Sachsenhausen, and, in 1941, transferred to Dachau where he remained until the end of the war.

The story of Martin Niemöller is by now well known in the English-speaking world. After the war, he served on the executive committee of the World Council of Churches, becoming president of that international body in 1961. He also became in the postwar period a leading voice in opposition to the rearmament of Germany. At the time of his death at age ninety-two, he was recognized as one of the principal voices on behalf of world peace and nuclear arms control.

The story behind these letters, however, is that of an earlier period in Niemöller's life, a period which found Pastor Niemöller in an intense struggle with his conscience, his vocation, and the destiny of his country. These letters are par-

1

ticularly important because they make available to English readers an insight into that struggle during its formative period as Niemöller unveiled it to those closest to him: his family and most intimate friends.

I

Since almost a half century has passed since Martin Niemöller wrote these letters, they should be placed and understood in their historical context before they are read. That context remains the subject of fierce debate in scholarly circles, even in the present period. Enough of its essential features are known, however, to permit a few observations that will aid the reader in understanding both the personal and national trauma of that time in Germany.

Martin Niemöller's struggle took place in the midst of a larger conflict within the German churches—both Catholic and Protestant—that to a large degree was precipitated by the Nazi seizure of power on January 30, 1933. That year marked the 450th anniversary of the birth of Martin Luther, and the events which transpired were in many ways as intense as those which initiated the great Reformation of the sixteenth century.

Most German Christians—both clerics and laity—greeted the appointment of Adolf Hitler as reichschancellor with mild to unrestrained enthusiasm. This number includes many of those who would subsequently come to oppose him. It includes Martin Niemöller. The reasons for this widespread support are not difficult to discern. Although the National Socialist party never won a popular majority in any free election in Germany, Hitler himself commanded immense popularity. He was seen as the strong leader whose devotion to restoring the national honor and prestige of Germany was beyond reproach. Hitler evoked the deepest yearnings of a people demoralized by their disastrous defeat in World War I and by the ostensible dishonor imposed on Germany by the Treaty of Versailles. He voiced the great resentment of a nation which came to find scapegoats for all of its problems—inflation, unemployment, political instability—in the Jews and communists.

But as the world now knows, Adolf Hitler was more than

a strong leader endowed with the extraordinary charismatic capacity to sway the masses. He was also a man possessed by an ideology which had as its aim the total transformation of the mind and life of the German nation and its people. From the outset, Hitler was single-mindedly committed to the creation of a genuine totalitarian state, one in which every institution in Germany—educational, social, cultural, industrial, political, and religious—would be "harmonized" or "coordinated" into a single purpose. That purpose was set forth in the creed of German National Socialism, with all of its glorification of the master race idea, its sense of a manifest destiny for the German nation, and its insane hatred of anything and everything Jewish.

Hitler and National Socialism had to deal with the two major religious loyalties in Germany in 1933: German Catholics and their principal political arm, the Catholic Center party, and German Protestantism. In the months immediately following Hitler's appointment as reichschancellor, it appeared the Catholic clergy might offer a significant center of opposition. When Hitler called a general election barely a month after coming to power in order to try to consolidate his strength in the German Parliament, the German Catholic bishops issued pastoral letters on the eve of the election that were virtually unanimous in their condemnation of National Socialism. The reign of terror unleashed by the Nazi brownshirts, which was felt by Catholics along with trade unionists, Social Democrats, and all other potential political opponents, was sufficient to cause Adolf Cardinal Bertram, archbishop of Breslau and chairman of the Conference of German Catholic Bishops, to express to President Hindenburg five days after the March election "the growing concern and fears of the Catholic populace" over what he described as "the precipitate events of recent days."

Tragically, however, most of the German Catholic bishops shortly shifted their position; they did not remain firm in their opposition to National Socialism. Barely four months later, the Vatican and the National Socialist government signed a concordat that, for all practical purposes, ended any prospect of major opposition from the Catholic church. From that point until the end of the war, the story of Catholic resistance is the courageous story of priests, nuns, and Catholic laypersons who took stances as individuals which the church was unwilling to take as an institution.

In German Protestantism, Hitler faced a complex history and a labyrinthine organizational structure that defies easy summary. In 1933, German Protestantism was divided into at least three major historical-confessional traditions and some twenty-eight separate administrative districts. During the decade prior to the Nazi seizure of power, these diverse creedal and regional churches had managed to achieve some semblance of union in the German Evangelical Federation of Churches. The federation was designed to allow for the careful expression of creedal differences while achieving some degree of administrative coordination, particularly in the areas of religious education, charities, and church-state relationships.

Hitler and National Socialism found many enthusiastic supporters among pastors and laity alike across the federation spectrum. But the unlimited enthusiasm of many who came to call themselves "German Christians" began, quite early, to create deep rifts within the Protestant fold. The Nazi party's unconcealed support for the German Christians, together with Hitler's crude attempts to forge the various confessions and regional churches into a single Reich church, brought matters rapidly to open conflict. Martin Niemöller, the virtually unknown pastor of St. Anne's Church in suburban Berlin, quickly became one of the principal leaders in that conflict.

The specific events which catapulted Niemöller into a position of prominence in what became known as the German church struggle took place during the spring and summer months of 1933. During this period, Hitler was publicly giving repeated assurance of his support for the churches. Two days after his appointment, for example, in his first radio address to the German people, the reichschancellor proclaimed that

> the national government will support and defend the foundations on which the strength of our nation is built. It will seek firmly to protect Christianity as the basis of our whole morality and the family as the nucleus of the life of our people and our community.[1]

4

But the actions of the national government would soon begin to prove otherwise.

Late in April, Hitler and the National Socialists took two actions that precipitated the first open breach between the government and the Protestant churches. On April 22, one of Hitler's more aggressive regional Nazi officials decided to appoint a state commissioner for the Evangelical church in the small province of Mecklenburg. That appointment produced a wave of protests from church leaders throughout Germany who were appalled by the state's undisguised usurpation of power in the internal affairs of the church. Letters and telegrams of protest were sent to Hindenburg, Hitler, and the minister of the interior which ultimately resulted in the appointment being withdrawn.

Far more serious was Hitler's appointment, on April 25, of a nondescript Army chaplain as his special advisor on church affairs. Ludwig Müller, his appointee, had little to commend him for such an important post beyond the fact that he was an ardent Nazi and an equally fervent German Christian. In a conversation with Müller a week before his appointment, Hitler gave him the specific assignment to further all efforts for the establishment of a single Evangelical German Reich church.

Such efforts, in fact, were already under discussion in the German Evangelical Church Federation. But the appointment of Müller, who promptly intruded himself into the midst of the discussions, triggered an immediate debate over who would be, as Reich bishop, the first head of the national church. Müller, who had the unanimous support of the German Christians, was nominated at a meeting of German Christian district leaders on May 23. The following day, the church federation committee which had prepared the constitution for the new church placed in nomination the name of Friederich von Bodelschwingh, a pastor widely respected by church leaders across the nation. Thus, the battle was joined.

A frenetic series of events took place over the next few months. Bodelschwingh was elected Reich bishop, the president of the German Evangelical Church Federation resigned because of ill health, and the minister of the interior appointed a lawyer as state commissioner for all the Evangelical churches in Prussia, the largest and most prestigious of the twenty-eight regional churches. The new commissioner, August Jäger, was not known to possess any personal qualities for such a sensitive post; a fellow attorney described him by saying he had never met a man who could rival Jäger in narrowness, presumption, arrogance, and meanness. True to form, Jäger dismissed the leading church officials of the church in Prussia, including the venerable church superintendent, Otto Dibelius, and replaced them with loyal German Christians. On the very day of Jäger's appointment, Bodelschwingh resigned as Reich bishop, and Müller, soundly defeated in the first election, proceeded to declare himself Reich bishop elect.

Matters came rapidly to a head in July, when general church elections were called on the 23rd to select the new representatives and officials of the reorganized church. The German Christians, aided by the government press, the ever-present agitation of the brownshirts, and by a personal national radio appeal by Hitler himself, won two-thirds of the elected positions. The new German Evangelical church was thus firmly in the hands of the German Christians and, consequently, of the National Socialist state.

In large measure, these were the events which brought about the church struggle and which brought a small group of German pastors, among them Martin Niemöller, to the fore. Although Niemöller had been among those who strongly supported the formation of the new Reich church and had in fact expressed the hope that it would bring about "a new meeting between our nation and the Christian church, between our nation and God," he, with others, became quickly alarmed by the efforts within the provincial churches to reorganize themselves under the new church constitution. Niemöller and his colleagues were especially disturbed by the radical change in the spiritual climate of the churches. Delegates to church synod meetings would frequently attend wearing the brownshirt uniforms of the S.A. (the National Socialist militia), complete with riding boots, swastikas, and military medals. Formal church meetings ended with prayer, the singing of Luther's hymn "A Mighty Fortress Is our God"—and the singing of the repulsive Horst Wessel song. A Swedish newspaper, reporting on such a spectacle at the meeting of the church synod of Brandenburg, concluded:

> The whole thing could only be described as religious barbarism. And the impression was not improved when the reporter was twice challenged in the hallway because he had neglected to give the Hitler salute.[2]

Particularly odious to Niemöller and others was the decision of one of the church's most powerful synods to adopt the infamous Aryan paragraph as one of its guiding regulations. A church adaptation of the government's civil service law of April 7, the Aryan paragraph provided for the ordination only of persons of Aryan descent and for the discharge of all clergy married to non-Aryans. Specifically aimed at the grand total of thirty-seven Protestant pastors in all of Germany in 1933 who were of Jewish descent, this act led to Niemöller's first organized effort on behalf of the opposition.

II

On September 21, 1933, two weeks after the synod that adopted the Aryan paragraph, Niemöller sent a circular letter to all German pastors, inviting them to join "an Emergency League of Ministers" who would give written assurances to one another that they would be bound only by the traditional creeds of the church in exercising their pastoral offices and that they would oppose the implementation of the Aryan paragraph. The response was immense. Within ten days, over 2,300 joined the Pastors' Emergency League. Four months later, over 7,000 of Germany's 18,000 Protestant pastors were members.

The league's initial act was to issue a statement of protest to the first national synod of the new church which met at Wittenberg on September 23 in a moment fraught with historic symbolism. Wittenberg was Martin Luther's burial place and the site at which, some four centuries earlier, he had nailed his famed ninety-five theses to the door of the castle church. The league statement was no less a theological treatise; it denounced the silencing of the dissenting minorities in the church by the German Christians, appealed for the rejection of the Aryan paragraph, and demanded that the national synod declare itself in support of the "unfettered preaching of the gospel." In an act of historic symbolism all its own, Niemöller and others posted copies of the statement on trees throughout Wittenberg.

The league mounted other protests of this sort as the situation within the church, from the league's perspective, continued to deteriorate. With Niemöller as its chief spokesman, the league continuously opposed the increasing alignment of the Evangelical church with National Socialism. It made its protests directly to Reich Bishop Müller, demanding that he discharge church officials who participated in some of the more outlandish displays of excessive nationalism and anti-Semitism. Pastors who were members of the league read denunciations of the church government from their pulpits and, in the early months of the movement, were successful in forcing from office some of the worst of the German Christian hierarchy. Strangely, the national government never banned the league, and although its members declined dramatically as National Socialism increased its stranglehold on German life, the league continued in existence throughout the entire period of the Third Reich.

The Pastors' Emergency League was to be the first of many opposition efforts which Niemöller either led or participated in. On January 24, 1934, Niemöller joined a delegation of church leaders who met with Hitler to protest some of the decrees of the Reich bishop, a meeting characterized by "heated" exchanges between Niemöller and Hitler; Niemöller told Hitler that church leaders had a God-given responsibility toward the German people. Four months later, Niemöller was one of the leading spirits in the organization of the famed Barmen synod at which church representatives of over 800,000 German Protestants issued a declaration that denounced the totalitarian aims of National Socialism. Two years later, Niemöller was one of ten signatories to a memorandum submitted to Hitler on behalf of the council of the Evangelical church. Among other items, the memorandum stated its direct condemnation of the government's early efforts to foster anti-Semitism among the German populace.

Neither Niemöller nor his pastoral colleagues, however, represented the whole or, as time passed, even a significant part of the general Protestant attitude toward Hitler and National Socialism. The church struggle was, in fact, a two-pronged battle. It was partly a conflict waged by elements of the clerical leadership and laity against National Socialism, but it also represented a struggle within the German Evangelical church among those who were loyal and enthusiastic supporters of Hitler and those who opposed him.

As a leader of the opposition, Niemöller's activities did not escape the attention of the government. He was periodically suspended, reinstated, and resuspended by the Reich bishop; at one point he was placed on permanent retirement— an action which Niemöller's congregation denounced and Niemöller himself ignored. On the very evening of his personal encounter with Hitler, Niemöller's rectory was ransacked by the gestapo, and a few days later a homemade bomb exploded in the rectory hall. It was, quite clearly, only a matter of time before the government took sterner measures with Pastor Niemöller.

Those measures came on July 1, 1937, at 8:30 A.M., when two gestapo agents came to Niemöller's rectory and asked him to accompany them to gestapo headquarters. Niemöller's biographer takes up the story:

> Arrived at their destination, the Gestapo men took Niemöller inside and told him to wait. The expected interrogation never took place. Instead, after waiting some hours, Niemöller was told to get back into the police van and was taken to the re-mand prison in Moabit. There his personal particulars were recorded, all his valuables were removed and he was put in a cell. With one small window high up in the wall and a squint-hole in the door, the cell was bare except for a table, stool, mess-tin and a bed of planks hinged against the wall which, as Niemöller was repeatedly warned, might be let down and used only at night. But he was dog-tired and so, as soon as the door was shut and bolted, he lay down on the concrete floor just as he was, in coat, collar and tie, and slept.[3]

Niemöller was kept at the Moabit prison for eight months. His trial began on February 7, 1938, and the court rendered its decision on March 2. The court found him guilty of a number of offenses, including causing a breach of the peace and "malicious and provocative criticism of the Ministers of Propaganda and Public Enlightenment (Dr. Goebbels), Education (Dr. Rust), and Justice (Dr. Gürtner)." Surprisingly, however, he was sentenced to seven months detention and a fine of 2,000 marks. The term of detention was remitted in light of the more than seven months Niemöller had already spent in prison. Niemöller, therefore, was a free man.

Tragically, the story did not end there. Niemöller was taken back to his cell to collect his personal effects before going home. "Late that night," his biographer recounts, "after he had waited in vain for his freedom, two gestapo officers in plain clothes took him by private car to the concentration camp at Sachsenhausen." He was imprisoned there and later at Dachau until the end of the war.

III

The letters which appear in this volume are translations from the German edition of Martin Niemöller's prison correspondence written during his eight-month confinement at Moabit prison. The German edition, edited by Niemöller's brother, Wilhelm, contains every piece of correspondence during that period which Niemöller wrote and which could be recovered. As Niemöller received literally thousands of pieces of mail during his imprisonment and, in many instances, found himself offering similar reassurances to many inquirers regarding the state of his health or on the spiritual importance of the struggle in which the church was engaged, it seemed best for the purposes of this English edition to select a representative sample of his voluminous correspondence. The letters included here seek to capture the nature of his concerns, his emotional and spiritual outlook, and the character of the issues and personalities that preoccupied his thoughts during this traumatic period. Letters that are rendered only in part contain ellipses to mark the omissions.

The reader who is not familiar with the detailed events of the church struggle should anticipate several characteristics of this correspondence. First, and as one would expect, the letters are intensely personal. Most were written by Niemöller to his wife, Else, and are filled with inquiries about the Niemöller children, close relatives and colleagues, and contain numerous expressions of concern for his wife's state of mind and for the affairs of his parish. The letters give us occasional glimpses of a man who is in immense personal turmoil, but who must constantly reassure his family and friends that he is well and who must reinforce their (and his own) conviction that the conflict which led to his arrest is a righteous cause— while struggling with his own uncertainties and doubts as to what may lie ahead.

Second, we get some insight into why Niemöller has been such a controversial figure throughout most of his career. These letters clearly reveal him as a man who does not bite his tongue. When he turns his attention to the conflict within the German Evangelical church itself, rather than the affairs of his own parish, he is as merciless in his characterization of several prominent church leaders whom he saw as vacillating on the key issues of the church struggle as he is tender and compassionate in his comments and quips about others in his circle of colleagues and acquaintances. Niemöller was often criticized at the time for his abrasiveness and his uncompromising stance. We see both traits of character in these exchanges with his family and clerical associates.

Third, and especially vexing for the nonspecialist, there are a significant number of references to persons, situations, and events that will have little meaning for those who are almost a half century removed from the period itself. Some of the references are nevertheless intriguing as, for example, Niemöller's cryptic greeting to Hermann Göring's sister (the letter of October 27), who was a quiet supporter of both Niemöller and the opposition movement in the church. Other references are to obscure or, in some instances, unknown persons. Some of the letters which contain these references have been included in this English edition because they are so clearly a part of Niemöller's principal concerns during this period, because they provide a profile of the innumerable German pastors and lay persons who were engaged in what— from the perspective of the German state—was treasonous activity, and because the tenderness, the humor, or the out-rage with which Niemöller writes—even when the references are obscure—are inextricable elements in the essence of the man himself.

To provide some assistance to the reader, the letters in this English edition have been kept in the chronological order in which they were written. They have been grouped into five sections, each one roughly corresponding to the concerns that appear to be uppermost in Niemöller's mind. Accordingly, Part One consists chiefly of letters of concern regarding his family and his parish. While the bulk of the letters throughout the German and English editions were written to his wife, this section is particularly expressive of Niemöller's anguish over the plight of his family.

In Part Two, Niemöller's attention turns more directly to his colleagues in the church struggle. His tone is lighter, his remonstrances are more forceful, and we can see that even though in prison, he is determined to continue to give lead-ership, guidance, and spiritual encouragement to the various efforts of the opposition movement within the church.

Part Three contains his Christmas correspondence. Early in November 1937, Niemöller and his attorneys initiated sev-eral attempts to have him released long enough to spend Christmas with his family. The letters in this section reveal, in a most touching manner, the restrained hope, the guarding against too much optimism, and finally the despair of that effort.

In Part Four, Niemöller has clearly recovered from the disappointment over his unsuccessful attempt to gain a Christ-mas furlough. He becomes lighthearted—even jovial—about the whole tragic business and begins, with his attorneys, to prepare for his forthcoming trial. Part Five contains eight let-ters written during the course of the trial and while Niemöller awaited its verdict. The last letter to his brother was written the day before the verdict was announced and he was trans-ported to the concentration camp at Sachsenhausen.

Each section is prefaced by a brief commentary that seeks to provide additional insight on the historical and, in some instances, technical background of the letters. The numbered footnotes are translations of Wilhelm Niemöller's notes in the

German edition; those marked by asterisks are notes provided by the editor and translators. Most Scripture passages are taken from the New English Bible, except in some instances in the text of the letters where Niemöller was clearly paraphrasing or quoting from memory.

IV

Finally, we return to the question raised at the outset of this Introduction: whether these letters might have any significance for readers other than those to whom they were originally addressed. As noted earlier, in the aftermath of the collapse of the Third Reich Martin Niemöller became simultaneously one of the most widely revered and controversial religious figures of modern times. But this fact alone, while it supports the effort to make known as much about him as possible, is not a sufficiently compelling reason to offer to English readers a selection of Niemöller's personal correspondence from such a brief—albeit tumultuous—period in his life. There is, in fact, a much more compelling reason.

Like the period in which Niemöller wrote, ours is also a time in which ideology, totalitarianism, and the struggles of consciences are not—or most certainly should not be— strangers to us. Ours, too, is a time of increasing international complexity and upheaval; it is also one in which incredibly simple political answers are being offered to immensely difficult problems.

Political violence and terrorism were not invented by the Nazis, and neither phenomenon disappeared with their defeat. The pathological ends of racism in the past half century have not been witnessed on a scale that approaches Hitler's "final solution" of the Jewish question, but the fact that such a solution to the persistent problem of race was once actually executed and with such barbarous, technological efficiency and inexplicable popular acquiescence cannot but grip the sensibilities of every thinking person alive today. Totalitarian regimes—whether of the left or the right—present a continuing threat to lovers of human freedom in our age as well.

In the midst of our own contemporary travails, therefore,

these letters can be read as an intimate glimpse into the private world of a man who was forced to confront many of the same issues which gnaw at the fragile fabric of civilized life in our generation. Not only is it possible but it is perhaps also imperative that we read Niemöller's thoughts and his experience as a commentary on his time . . . and on our own.

ON THEOLOGICAL REFLECTION AND ETHICAL COMMITMENT

In Martin Niemöller's experience we discern a critical distinction between the nature and consequences of theological reflection and the imperatives of ethical commitment. Niemöller was not a theologian. Unlike the famous martyr of the church struggle, Dietrich Bonhoeffer, Niemöller's prison experience did not produce a major theological literature or tradition. Both were men of deep religious faith, both were men of action, and both felt compelled to act on the basis of their commitment to a set of beliefs and their participation in a community that, for them, transcended the narrow boundaries of nation, race, and political creed.

Niemöller's religious beliefs, however, were not the outcome of coolly dispassionate theological deliberations. They were convictions calcined in the crucible of his day-to-day experience. And that experience, in turn, confirmed and reinforced his beliefs. An illustration helps make this distinction clear.

Both Bonhoeffer and Niemöller took early exception to the notorious Aryan paragraph by which the German Christians joined the national government in their effort to exclude pastors of Jewish ancestry from the Christian clergy. Bonhoeffer's response was to write a lengthy theological treatise in which he examined both the political and ecclesiastical consequences of this exclusionary attempt. To his credit, Bonhoeffer perceived that the Aryan paragraph, if taken seriously, would have implications not only for pastors of Jewish background but for Jewish converts to Christianity as well. He also perceptively took to task "the very criterion of race" as a principle of national policy. But he shied away, as his biographer notes, from taking any personal action—at this point in the struggle—which might endanger the relationships between the church and the state.

For Niemöller, however, the Aryan paragraph was a matter for immediate and direct response. When a Nazi-inspired questionnaire was circulated among the clergy, asking them to identify their racial ancestry, Niemöller—as one of his first directives issued through the Pastors' Emergency League— called upon the pastors to ignore it. The continual agitation of the league on this and other issues during the fall of 1933 was sufficiently disquieting that Reich Bishop Müller, in January of the following year, issued a "Decree for the Restoration of Orderly Conditions in the German Evangelical Church." The "muzzle decree," as it came to be called, forbade any criticism of "the church government or its actions publicly or by distributing statements, especially flyers." The league, under Niemöller's leadership, reacted immediately by issuing just such a flyer—which was read from some 3,500 pulpits over the following two Sundays. The declaration denounced the attempt to interfere with the freedom of the pulpit, asserted the illegality of Müller's decree, and ended with the strident pronouncement:

> Where the bishops teach, maintain, or uphold something contrary to the gospel, we have God's command in such a case not to obey. One should also not follow properly elected bishops when they are in error.[4]

Niemöller's resistance was instinctive and public. Of course, neither the stature nor the quality of Bonhoeffer's ultimate sacrifice is diminished by pointing out that he agonized up until the outbreak of the war over the question of his personal role and responsibility in the battle with the state. Whatever Niemöller's doubts were, they vanished early; his critics would call him "impetuous" and shake their heads at his lack of diplomacy in his encounters with church and Nazi officials— including Hitler himself. For Martin Niemöller to have convictions was to express them in direct, concrete act on.

ON RELIGION AND POLITICS

Niemöller and his fellow leaders in the church struggle were accused after the war of having focused their attention on too narrow a set of issues. Their opposition, the claim went, grew out of a parochial concern for the integrity and independence of the church; it never expanded to consider the demonic consequences of National Socialism generally as it imposed its will on other segments of German society.

As Niemöller, Karl Barth, and others would themselves acknowledge after the war, such criticisms were tragically valid. But they do not eclipse the significance of the church struggle itself for what was at stake, at least in part, was the issue of how the church would respond to the attempt to forge a new bond between government and religion, the state and the church, theology and politics.

Among the Nazis, the question of religion and politics was one on which attitudes were decidedly mixed. Some, like Alfred Rosenberg, thought that a "pure" Christianity, shorn of its Jewish underpinnings, could become a vital element in the establishment of the new order. Others, such as General Ludendorff, Hitler's comrade-in-arms in the abortive Munich putsch of 1923, were fanatically committed to the downfall of Christianity as an obstacle to the totalitarian aims and ends of Nazism. Hitler proved to be the consummate pragmatist on the issue. He needed the churches only so long as he needed, in the early months of his regime, to consolidate his political power and the institutional bases of his appeal to the German masses. Once the latter was accomplished he was fully committed, as he is reported to have said on one occasion, to let the church "rot like a gangrenous limb."

For the churches, the desire to develop a new relationship between church and state was driven by two common fears which united Catholics and Protestants alike: their abhorrence of communism and their perception of the rampant immorality of the era. Both fears were by-products of Germany's brief and tragic experiment with democratic liberalism—the period of the Weimar Republic—which followed Germany's defeat in World War I and preceded the Nazi rise to power. The Weimar period was the crucible in which the attitudes of both the churches and the Nazi state were formed.

The Weimar Republic has been described as a tacit acknowledgment that there were in reality, two Germanies:

the Germany of military swagger, abject submission to authority, aggressive foreign adventure, and obsessive preoccupation with form, and the Germany of lyrical poetry, humanistic philosophy and pacific cosmopolitanism.[5]

The churches were part and parcel of the first Germany, the Germany of militarism, authoritarianism, and conservatism. What they saw in the Weimar period was not a cultural breath of fresh air or the flowering of a new spirit of political and intellectual freedom. They saw, instead, a wind of change that was rank with the odor of left-leaning socialism, Bolshevism, and moral decay. Where Germany's progressive elite saw, in the words of the poet Rilke, "the ardent hope that mankind would for once turn over a new page," the churches were among those who saw only

> a country of modernism and freedom [and a] freedom degenerated into licence. . . . Bars for homosexuals, cafes where men danced with men, new liberty between the sexes, nudism, camping, sun-bathing, pornographic literature in the corner kiosks.[6]

Because Hitler and National Socialism promised an end to these evils, they found widespread support among the Protestant and Catholic masses. Even the church hierarchy, which denounced Nazism on other grounds, was quite willing to accept and applaud its determination to stop the communist menace and to restore a climate of moral rectitude in the nation.

The process of national restoration—or more accurately, the counterrevolution—did not consist only in the consolidation of political power by the Nazis. It was a process of cultural transformation aided and abetted, with unrestrained enthusiasm, by the right wing of the German Evangelical church—the "German Christians," as they called themselves. For this segment of the church, National Socialism as a political creed and the Nazi party as a political movement became vehicles through which their most deeply felt values and intensely held convictions could be transformed into national policy. Crude cultural sentiments historically held in check by the fractured creedal and administrative structure of German

17

Protestantism found both a channel and an opportunity for expression in the excessive nationalistic climate of Nazism.

The German Christians had begun to organize themselves on the eve of the Nazi political triumph in January 1933. The German Christian Movement, organized in 1930 by a Prussian pastor, was dedicated to combating "free thinkers, socialists, communists, and pacifists." It was joined by the Faith Movement of German Christians, formed two years later, in working to kindle an interest in politics and national renewal within the church.

The enthusiasm with which such movements undertook this challenge was virtually without restraint. Pastor Joachim Hossenfelder, Reich leader of the Faith Movement group, declared the German Christians to be "the S.A. [that is, the brownshirts] of Jesus Christ. . . . We regard as holy these laws of God's creation: marriage, family, race, people, state, and authority." In its first national assembly in April 1933, following a succession of speeches calling for the integration of church and politics, the Faith Movement passed a resolution which stated in part:

> God has created me a German. Germanism is a gift of God; God desires that I battle for my Germanism. . . . The church is, for a German, a communion of believers that is duty bound to fight for a Christian Germany. The goal of the German Christian Faith Movement is one evangelical German church. The state of Adolf Hitler calls for such a church; the church must hear that call.[7]

In reaction to such admixtures of Christianity and politics, Niemöller and his fellow pastors in the Emergency League and later in the Confessing church took their stand. Because the "error" of the German Christians was seen as a fundamentally theological one, it was answered first in the stern theological language of Karl Barth, then professor of theology at the University of Bonn. In a pamphlet published the same day that Bodelschwingh resigned as Reich bishop, Barth wrote:

> The mighty temptation of our age is that we no longer appreciate the intensity and exclusiveness of the demand of the divine Word . . . so that in our anxiety in the face of existing

dangers we no longer put our whole trust in the authority of God's Word, but think we ought to come to its aid with all sorts of contrivances.[8]

In this simple declaration, replete with the language peculiar to the Protestant tradition and its understanding of the relationship between the church and holy Scripture, Barth set in motion the effort of opposition which Niemöller and others would mount against the attempt to harmonize and integrate the Christian faith and politics. That effort would ultimately lead to a raging battle over which segment of German Protestantism constituted the "true church"—the German Christians or the Confessing church which emerged from the historic synod at Barmen, May 1934. Niemöller led the organizational efforts of the Confessing church; Barth would later say of him,

> When I think of Martin Niemöller, I think of him as the embodiment of "Barmen." . . . Pastor Niemöller in the Dahlem congregation was and is exemplary for the "Church Struggle."[9]

But it was Barth himself who would draw the theological line between the realm of the church and the affairs of politics that would prove decisive in the battle which Niemöller spearheaded:

> State and Church have to recognize in each other the distinct authority given to them and also to keep it within the limits set for them. But a coordination of Church and State ignores and confuses the nature and task of the State . . . and the Church. . . . Therefore, we condemn . . . making the State into a Church *or the Church into a State.*[10] (emphasis added)

Clearly, then, the anxiety of a great many Germans in the 1930s over the threat of communism, the perceived lax morals of the times, the state of the economy, and the loss of national honor represented in Germany's defeat in World War I and the subsequent Treaty of Versailles impelled the right wing of the German Evangelical church toward an interest in politics in general and National Socialist politics in particular. By banding forces with the political sphere, these German Christians, for whom religious faith and national patriotism were indistinguishable, sought to consecrate as national policy their own tragic understanding of the cultural, social, and racial dimensions of their Christian faith.

In so doing, they made two fatal errors. They failed to recognize that their right-wing version of Christianity was useful to National Socialism only because it meshed with National Socialism's own right-wing ideologies. Hitler needed the German Christians to legitimate his appeal to the German populace; once entrenched in power, he quite readily abandoned his attempts to control the church through a manipulation of its internal structure and leadership, and simply imposed an external, governmental reichsminister for church affairs to handle the churches as one of the many bureaucratic chores which the government had to manage.

The second error was the greater one. As Niemöller, Barth, and others saw from the beginning, the effort (in Barth's words) to "coordinate Church and State" could lead only to a monumental perversion of the church and everything for which it stood. Not until the end of the war would the whole of Germany, including the church, come to realize how great that perversion had been. Thus, something slightly more than prophetic sounds in the penultimate paragraph of a memorandum which Martin Niemöller and nine other leaders of the Confessing church sent to Hitler on June 4, 1936, barely a year before Niemöller's arrest. It stated,

> We beg . . . that our people may be free to pursue their way in the future under the sign of the cross of Christ, that our grandchildren may not one day curse the fathers for having built up a state on the earth for them and left it behind, but shut them out of the Kingdom of God.[11]

ON RELIGION, TOTALITARIANISM, AND RESISTANCE

George F. Kennan, one of postwar America's most distinguished statesmen, once made an extraordinarily astute comment regarding totalitarianism:

> I suspect, furthermore, that a neurotic sense of tidiness in political arrangements can be a great danger in any society. Too great an urge for symmetry and order, too strong an insistence on uniformity and conformity, too little tolerance for

the atypical and minority phenomenon: these are all things that can grease the path by which nations slide into totalitarianism.

[We Americans have been lucky] up to this time, with our sectional diversities, our checks and balances, and our deference to the vital interests of competing minorities. Woe to any of us, if these things begin to yield to the leveling influences of the perfectionist, to utopian dreams of progress and equality, to the glorification of conformity in tongue or outlook that have been embraced in the concept of romantic nationalism and have gone before the disasters of totalitarian triumph. Diversity, in all the glorious disorder of nature, is the best defense of healthy societies.[12]

In the final analysis, Martin Niemöller may be seen as one of the enduring symbols of diversity in a society which demanded only order, symmetry, and uniformity. He is a symbol that does not permit itself to be idolized; Niemöller, too, was a religious conservative at heart and an ardent nationalist in spirit. Like nearly every German who lived through the era of the Third Reich, Niemöller had moments during this period in his life when his response to National Socialism was less than commendable. But reading his overall record, in the light of his time and our own—his insistence on maintaining the faith and freedom of the church, his unwillingness to see either fettered by ostensibly higher claims, the fearlessness with which he spoke his mind, even his "impetuosity"—makes him one of the rare examples of courage in one of history's grimmest eras.

Genuine courage and integrity are rare commodities in any age; real acts of resistance must be measured against the threat which the resistor confronts and the alternatives that are available. As an act of resistance, Martin Niemöller's stance can be judged by the eight years in prison and concentration camps which his courage cost him. Others during this period paid for their courage with their lives. From each of them and from their experiences with the German Third Reich, our generation and future generations may learn something of the fate in store for an otherwise civilized society that succumbs to extremism in politics, its endorsement by religion, and the acceptance of both by a disillusioned populace.

1. J. S. Conway, *The Nazi Persecution of the Churches: 1933–45* (New York: Basic Books, 1968), p. 15.

2. Ibid., p. 47.

3. Dietmar Schmidt, *Pastor Niemöller,* trans. Lawrence Wilson (Garden City, N.Y.: Doubleday, 1959), p. 102.

4. Ernst C. Helmreich, *The German Churches Under Hitler* (Detroit: Wayne State University Press, 1979), p. 154.

5. Peter Gay, *Weimar Culture* (New York: Harper & Row, 1968), p. 1.

6. T. L. Jarman, *The Rise and Fall of Nazi Germany* (New York: New American Library, 1961), p. 117.

7. Conway, *Nazi Persecution,* p. 31.

8. In Arthur C. Cochrane, *The Church's Confession Under Hitler* (Philadelphia: Westminster, 1962), p. 102.

9. Ibid., p. 110.

10. Ibid., pp. 125–6.

11. Ibid., p. 278.

12. George F. Kennan, "Totalitarianism and Freedom," in Carl J. Friedrich, ed., *Totalitarianism* (Cambridge: Harvard University Press, 1954), p. 29.

PART I
July 2, 1937
through
November 8, 1937

Niemöller's prison correspondence begins with a letter to his wife, written the day after his arrest. Compared with his later letters, this early correspondence is somewhat formalized, reflecting both the shock and strain of his initial confinement. He laments not hearing from his family (the letter of July 26), reassures his colleagues that he is managing his solitude (August 2), is buoyed by the flood of mail he begins to receive in August, but remonstrates with his wife for leaving his letters where they can be read by others (October 25). This personal correspondence reveals the persons of prominence who were supporters of the Confessing church, including the sister of Hermann Göring (the letter of October 27).

The names explained in the footnotes throughout the correspondence are a veritable roll call of leaders of the Confessing church, leaders to whom Niemöller either writes or continually refers throughout his eight months of confinement in Moabit. The indications of their subsequent fate dramatizes the lengths to which the government went in order to crush opposition among church leaders and laity to the aims of the German Third Reich.

July 2, 1937
To Mrs. Else Niemöller

Dear Else,

I'm sorry that I did not at least say goodbye to you yesterday, but at the moment I thought of everything else but the possibility that I would not be back after a few hours. Despite the bustle, I would have talked over a few things with you that I'm thinking about now—especially the children and the congregation's situation. The latter will now have to take care of itself without me. Instead of being a preacher I'll now have to be a defendant. And in the first twenty-four hours I have already learned a lot about being one. You can tell everyone at the church office, and anyone from the congregation who inquires, that I'm confident despite everything that might come, and that I hope to be ready if I'm led along paths which I would not have chosen by myself. I think a great deal about Christ's last words to Peter and—please pass this on to our good friend Hildebrandt; he used the same words at the communion right after the ordination of Vikarinnen in the Church of Jesus Christ in Dahlem when he pronounced a number of blessings that began "Fear Not!"—"I think you ought to think about these blessings now and be joyful: nothing can happen to me!"

As far as the matter at hand is concerned, I have the impression the congregation understands that the future can only be sustained with Christ's joyous message, and that truly it will work out with him. It's a good thing especially for me that I was able to preach in Bochum once again about "the salt of the earth and the light of the world" and that I was able to be really active during the last few weeks. I truly would like to have celebrated communion Monday night—but I'm content and thankful despite the nagging desires because I can now let myself be supported by him whom I have preached. How wonderful that this at least does not have to be relearned: the rock will stand and remain unmoved by anything we may encounter! Think of me when you read the daily lessons; I hope to be able to read them mornings and evenings—and let's not become impatient: love God and have patience in Christ! How often I have said it to newlyweds, and now I'm saying it to you and me! United with you in faith, I am faithfully,

Your Martin

July 23, 1937 [1]
To Mrs. Else Niemöller

. . . This postcard is to let you know that I am with you and the congregation in spirit every day—especially on Sundays— and that I am praying with you all for open ears, so that the word which our heavenly father lets us pronounce will prove its comforting, sustaining, and strengthening power through us! Right now I especially know how great a need we have for it and how in essence there is nothing but "God's Word and the prayer of Christians" as Luther once put it, and I thankfully confess that it has helped me find peace in all my timid reluctance and that it still helps me now daily. I think a lot about the others who have to go through the same vale with me, and if I have a request, it is for the congregation not to tire of intercession. . . .

1. On this same date, Niemöller's brother, Pastor Wilhelm Niemöller, was interrogated by the gestapo concerning the dissemination of
copies of Bishop Otto Dibelius's sermon delivered on July 4. Nothing
came of that interrogation, however. The gestapo preferred to concentrate
on its attempts to forbid or to prevent intercession on behalf of Martin
Niemöller and other prisoners. The custom of intercession was practiced
regularly by the Confessing congregations but not by "intact" or neutral
churches until the end of the war. Although it was frequently attacked, it
was never actually prohibited. When a special intercession service was held
for Niemöller and sixty-six other jailed pastors in the Dahlem church on
August 8, approximately 250 worshipers were arrested; two days later, 49
were still under arrest.

July 25, 1937[1]
To Mrs. Else Niemöller

. . . We should thank God for supporting me so, and for not
permitting any spirit of mourning into cell 448. The questions
Why? How long? To what end?—I'm of course familiar with
them, and occasionally they stick their head in the door. But
they are not allowed to stay. Hymn 198, verse 6: "Begone
you mournful spirits. . . . Jesus, my joy!" . . .

1. This was the fourth Sunday after Niemöller's arrest. His brother
Wilhelm preached three successive services at the Dahlem congregation
in order to accommodate all the congregants.

July 26, 1937
To Pastor Wilhelm Niemöller

My dear Wilhelm,
Unfortunately I have not heard from you all week, but at least at the beginning of a new one I want to send you heartfelt greetings. I believe it would be best if you kept in touch with me through Else; that way I can be sure to make contact at least once a week. You don't have to worry about me; to be sure everything is terribly uncertain but it's of value that I'm now attending the school where one learns what is written in Philippians 4:11–13.* I hope you and your loved ones are well and that the church in Westphalia is truly following the path of her forefathers! I have no news from our parents, but the last I heard sounded good—by the same token I assume Else's silence is a good sign. Give my greetings to our brethren in Bielefeld. How long can this period of trial last? It's a good thing we know who determines the shape of its beginning and end! My greetings to your Ingeborg and the children. I embrace you, your faithful brother,

Martin

My regards to the president[1] and Lücking[2] the next time you see them!

*"Not that I am alluding to want, for I have learned to find resources in myself whatever my circumstances. I know what it is to be brought low, and I know what it is to have plenty. I have been very thoroughly initiated into the human lot with all its ups and downs—fullness and hunger, plenty and want. I have strength for anything through Him who gives me power."

1. Dr. Karl Koch (b. 1876) was president of the Westphalian regional synod from 1927. From 1934 he was president of the Westphalian Confessing synod as well as president of the German Confessing synod.
2. Pastor Karl Lücking (b. 1893) was an active force in the West-

28

phalian Council of Brethren and the Pastors' Emergency League. In 1936, he became a member of the council of the German Evangelical church. In July 1938, he was arrested along with other members of the Council of Brethren and was banished to Jastrow in the Grenzmark. After the war, he was vice-president of the Evangelical church of Westphalia.

August 2, 1937
To Mrs. Else Niemöller

... I can't quarrel with the direction our life has taken, and you should not either—and probably don't. We can grasp with bare hands how faith, love, and hope in and around us are gaining fresh strength. And come what may, we want to look forward with faith: he can mean no harm. Where we are mindful of the word God has uttered to us we live in glory—certain in our faith and not in our sight, but in such a way that our faith becomes a living reality and we continue with Paul: "But we are confident." And thus through God's grace a day will come when we shall be given back to one another, and we will surely not have become poorer but richer (as in Colossians 1:24).* Wherever this is being divined in the church—and its concept is slowly being recognized again—seeds will sprout! It will come and through God's grace will then grow and bear fruit, and we and our children—if it might be so—we and our children shall rejoice in it. . . .

*"It is now my happiness to suffer for you. This is my way of helping to complete, in my poor human flesh, the full tale of Christ's afflictions still to be endured, for the sake of His body which is the church."

August 2, 1937
To Pastor Ernst Koenigs,[1] Weisel

My dear Ernst!
When my wife visited me today after a two-week lapse she brought your greetings and gave 2 Corinthians 6:4–10 as your message to me. This was a true joy and refreshment for me. I've now had four and a half weeks to get used to my solitude. The first few days were not easy, but since I've acquired a Bible and a hymnal, I've been using my time to the fullest and am amazed how fast it passes. Initially I had a few worries remembering the "cabin fever" during my years as a cadet and lieutenant before the war. I'm now learning patience—late but thoroughly—and it isn't in vain: every day I learn a few hymns and read Scripture calmly, deliberately, and with the question, "Lord, what would you have me do?" Because of this I've come to see the value of my time under arrest as a basis for manifold thanks. The congregation prays and has grown only closer to God's word. Who would not rejoice? I'm beginning to have a new understanding of Paul's Philippian letter: "Rejoice in the Lord always, and again I say rejoice." What becomes of me is in our Lord's hands. I am sure his way is right, wherever it may lead. My wife is healthy and brave. We thank one another for our common bond of faith. Greetings to your loved ones. I commend you to God.

Your old friend Martin

1. Pastor Ernst Koenigs (b. 1890) in Weisel (Hessen-Nassau); later an inmate of the concentration camp at Sachsenhausen from September 13, 1939, to December 15, 1940.

August 3, 1937
To Pastor Wilhelm Niemöller

My dear Wilhelm!

Last Sunday I received a mountain (170 pieces) of fairly dated mail.[1] The love of the congregation interrupted the trickle which brought the greetings of my family: "who was ever hurt by love. . . ." I just wanted to tell you that included was a postcard of yours dated July 10 and that I was glad to receive it despite its venerable age. In the meantime, of course, we have seen each other and talked;[2] it has even come to my attention that you stood in my pulpit a week ago Sunday—three times yet! On top of that, you acquainted yourself with Alex;[3] I was happy to hear of your quick release, not only for your sake but also that of our parents, especially father. An arrest is sometimes greater punishment for those who stay on the outside than it is for those who are inside!

At any rate, I'm doing well. Now, of course I have some things to "work on," that is, to think about, but if anything has become clear to me during the past four and a half weeks it is that in our situation it is not a question of "our case"[4] but that of our Lord Jesus. Should this not be cause for optimism? I have also received the greetings of the many brethren from the Ravensburg Council of Brethren; would you please convey my thanks?[5] Just recently I have noticed how matter-of-factly the mention of Paul's imprisonment in Caesarea reads (Acts 24:27): "When two years had passed . . ." as if it were nothing! Thus it won't be anything! Jesus' message will continue, it cannot be stopped. Barred doors will not stop it. My heartfelt greetings to you, Ingeborg, and the children, the brethren in office, and the congregation of Jacobus[6] which are expressed in the joy of community with the "eternal covenant," the subject of today's lesson (Genesis 17:7).

As always, your Martin

Else was here yesterday during visiting hours!
Just received your postcard of July 30—many, many thanks!

1. Niemöller received so much mail that a special censor had to be employed. The prisoner himself received permission to write twelve postcards a day—an amount which was later increased.

2. Wilhelm Niemöller (b. 1898), a pastor in Bielefeld and member of the Westphalian Council of Brethren, was permitted to visit Niemöller in the Moabit prison with his sister-in-law Else on July 17, 1937; later they went to the state prosecutor's office and to the attorney Dr. Horst Holstein.

3. Alexanderplatz, headquarters of the gestapo (see also note to the letter of July 23).

4. On August 8, Martin Niemöller's defense counsel requested a delay for his client in order to be able to review materials pertinent to his defense. . . . The request was denied.

5. The "greetings of the many brethren from Ravensburg" probably dates from July 5, 1937, when the confessing pastors from the synods of Bielefeld, Halle, and Herford were meeting in Unmelm.

6. The congregation in Bielefeld to which Wilhelm Niemöller was pastor.

August 3, 1937
To Miss Hermine Hermes[1]

Dear Miss Hermine Hermes,

Along with the last great mail delivery—in the future I have asked to have only letters from my immediate family forwarded here because nothing arrives even halfway on time—I received your dear note. My heartfelt thanks! I hope you can continue to get along in your work; it is probably much more difficult for you now that we men have fallen by the wayside. But in these terrible times, the church women are needed on the front and these have not been the worst of times. I'm doing fairly well; I have even recovered a little and gained some strength. To be sure, we can at this point only be upheld by the word of promise; it is there and we hear it: "Neither abandoned nor neglected!" . . . "What promises he makes, he keeps!" Please give my kindest regards to Miss Gottschalg[2] and any other acquaintances you come in contact with—some from the country perhaps! Yours in faithful, common bond of belief and service.

Martin Niemöller

1. Miss Hermine Hermes was secretary of the Pastors' Emergency League for the duration of the church struggle. She often had difficulties with the gestapo, but held out until the end. Thirty-four years afterwards, she wrote that she would not have been able to hold up had she not been able to always fall back on the help and advice of the president of the Brandenburg synod, Pastor Kurt Scharf.
2. Miss Gottschalg was the pastor's assistant and helped with the business management of the Pastors' Emergency League.

August 9, 1937[1]
To Mrs. Else Niemöller

. . . Once again I am writing down Calvin's word for you: "We should not think ourselves to be pitiable in a situation in which Jesus praises us blissfully with his own words" (Matthew 5:10). Today I am personally in this state: "My heart rejoices and I cannot be sad." I am also sure that this source of power and joy won't dry up because our prayer reopens its locks continually—how is it put in the beautiful church prayer: Lord, give us peace in our time, because no one fights for us but you, our God, alone! But that he does it should be enough for us, and how he does it we'll leave up to him! . . .

1. On August 8, Niemöller's attorney had protested his arrest to no avail.

August 12, 1937[1]
To Mrs. Else Niemöller,

. . . All my worries issued from outside, not from within. If I can think of you and the congregation without worry, I am master of all things and a joyous child of our father in heaven, despite my cell of four times 2.5 meters × 2.5 meters. Verily it is the truth of the gospel: Psalm 118:6.*

I'm really sorry for people who know nothing about it, truly sorry. Tell everyone that I'll do very well so long as all of you keep the faith firmly. You know that I stand for a good thing, that I have a clear conscience, and you ought to know that our Lord Jesus Christ will surely guide things in such a way that they will serve you, me, and the whole church for the best. . . .

*"The Lord is on my side, I have no fear; what can man do to me?"

1. On this date, the Council of Brethren informed the Westphalian Confessing synod of the arrest of 250 participants in the service of intercession held at the Church of Jesus Christ in Dahlem on August 8. In the same circular, it was noted that proceedings against Martin Niemöller had been scheduled for August 10, 12, and 16—but had been "temporarily postponed."

August 12, 1937
To Unknown

Dear young lady,

Your letter reached my hands, and I wish to answer that today I find myself—after six weeks in my cell—not only unbroken but thankful and rejoicing in God's merciful guidance. It is one of our Lord Jesus Christ's unfathomable kindnesses that his faithfulness will keep us balanced in all situations, truly "as if nothing had happened" precisely because everything of value to us in the present and hereafter has happened. Now I am taking a rest in peace away from the many disturbances of the last few years and wait confidently and patiently to see whether or not the Lord will require my services again outside these walls! Whether and when? That is not for me to worry! Please give my greetings to all of the Burckhardt house.[1] Along with the others whom God has placed in solitude and quiet, I know that I'm supported by numerous prayers! In today's lesson it is written: "Hear me, O Lord, for thy loving kindness is good!" (Psalm 69:16). In the fellowship of our faith,

Your Martin Niemöller

1. The Burckhardt house in Dahlem was a center for work directed toward young women. During this period it was directed by Pastor Otto Riethmüller (1889– 1938) who was elected a member of the Reich Council of Brethren during the German Evangelical church's Confessing synod held in Oeynhausen in February 1936.

August 16, 1937[1]
To Mrs. Else Niemöller

. . . Everything is simply marching in step; only the gospel—
praise God—moves forward according to other laws. . . .

1. August 16, 1937, was the third and last day which had been scheduled by the special court for the trial. There was no sign that preparation
for the trial caused the accused to be worried or excited. His counsel was
his trusted friend and attorney, Dr. Horst Holstein, about whom Hermann
Ehlers wrote an especially beautiful brief biographical portrait (see Wilhelm Niemöller, *Lebensbilder aus der Bekennenden Kirche* [Bielefeld, 1949]).
Holstein's colleague was assistant judge Dr. Herbert Wehrhahn, who, as
a faithful member of the Confessing church, gladly relinquished a part of
his vacation to prepare for the trial. Also engaged in the defense was the
attorney Dr. Hans Koch, who had just carried out an excellent defense of
Wilhelm von Arnim, Hermann Ehlers, Gerhard Jacobi, and Wilhelm Niesel during their trial on July 2. Dr. Willy Hahn, another attorney, had
already been retained for the defense on July 7. All three worked well
together during the subsequent trial and in later years until Hahn's death
in 1942, Koch's execution for his participation in the events of July 20,
1944, and Holstein's sudden death in November 1945. The idea that one
could suffer the trial silently without participating apparently did not occur
to Niemöller at this time, contrary to his attitude in February and March,
1938. It seemed clear to him that "everything was simply marching in
step."

August 16, 1937
To Pastor Hans Friedrich Lenz, Münzenberg[1]

Dear Brother Lenz!

By all rights today should have been the last day of the proceedings of my trial, and I had actually planned to return to my congregation and the circle of my family this evening. But that was not to be and the lesson of patience continues. But I am well and in good spirits, and I am slowly teaching myself to quit making plans and to quit listening to the plans of men. That is likely to be the intent of this examination! Instead I have time for more important things, and among them is to thank those who have sent greetings. That is why I want to tell you that brotherly love and intercession has constantly surrounded and strengthened me during these weeks. And our heavenly father has not let me lack what is needed: "I will praise God's work; I will put my faith in God, and I will not be afraid; how can flesh harm one?!" Body and soul have remained intact, and my heart, having been thrown at God's mercy, is full of confidence and joy. Greetings to the brethren.[2]

In faithfulness,
Your Martin Niemöller

1. Pastor Hans Friedrich Lenz (b. 1902) of Münzenberg, Upper Hessia.
2. A duplicate of this letter notes the names of 115 pastors and congregation members who were under arrest on August 11, 1937.

August 17, 1937
To Unknown

Dear Brother,
Many thanks to you and all of the Council of Brethren for your dear words of greeting and text. Even though it reached me with considerable delay, I have nevertheless received it and it has strengthened me. Indeed it completely represents my attitude toward what we are going through as the congregation of Jesus Christ: "So long as Christ is being proclaimed"—"as if nothing had happened!" Indeed, nothing has happened but his "sweet miracle" so dear to me, and we are its messengers—here or there, one way or the other! And so I can tell you of myself: I'm not suffering any depression or craving for revenge; instead I view this test—frankly it is also a burden—as punishment by our father. I view the quietude— frankly it is also a temptation—as a period of grace for listening and prayer. And thus far every day I have become and remain comforted and assured. 2 Corinthians 4:17–18.* This is a time of blessing for the church. With heart and faith,

                                                   Your Martin Niemöller

*"Our troubles are slight and short-lived; and their outcome an eternal glory which outweighs them far. Meanwhile our eyes are fixed, not on the things that are seen, but on the things that are unseen: for what is seen passes away; what is unseen is eternal."

August 18, 1937
To Mrs. Else Niemöller

. . . You don't have to worry about me; I live my day and it's never long, and should there be occasional rough weather and storms on the surface, at a diving depth of twenty meters there is total calm. God surely has worked us over, has put us to his blacksmith's forge, and yet has said to us and shown us again and again that his plans for us are only for the best. He will rest his bellows again at the right time and we will let him rule and do as he wishes, until as is his due, he with miraculous design completes the work which has caused you to worry. . . .

August 23, 1937
To Mrs. Else Niemöller

. . . Since our last meeting quite a bit has happened, some of it difficult.[1] But our Lord Jesus Christ has surely remained the same and will remain he who guides all according to his will. Thus we have to march after him; we will find out soon enough where he is taking us! And with the certainty that his path is the right one—always and under all conditions—I have made my way from one day to the next during these two months, and I never had to carry more than I was given the strength for. In contrast I have always been the one who was carried and have received much joy! This morning I read Philippians 2:14: "Do all you have to do without complaint or wrangling!" That must be where the secret is hidden. . . .

1. "Since our last meeting" probably refers to the visiting hour of Monday, August 9, to which Else brought their daughter Brigitte and her brother-in-law, Wilhelm Niemöller. "Some of it difficult" quite certainly does not simply allude to the postponement of the trial date. On August 11, the sorely tried Confessing church had to accept a new loss: Pastor Karl Immer of Barmen, father of the Confessing synods, had a stroke while under arrest at gestapo headquarters on Alexanderplatz. He remained partially paralyzed until his death in May 1944.

August 24, 1937
To Unknown[1]

My very dear young lady!
I've been wanting to thank you for your greeting for some time, but it has become an artistic accomplishment to get through as much love as I am surrounded with—as by a stream, and that stream carries the swimmer. What I have received by way of love during these past weeks will always stay in my heart—even if I should live to be a hundred years old. Unpleasant as being silenced has been and remains for me, as painfully as I am pressed by the thought of being declared "an enemy" by my own people,[2] as much as I am wracked by my concern for what the responsible church leaders will or won't do in the face of the catastrophe which is revealing itself, I must praise God every day and thank him for being true to his promise! Today's word, Isaiah 12:4, comes therefore once again out of the fullness of my heart. Pity the people who don't know it, and a lazy church which does not shout it constantly! "We should praise God every day and thank his name forever!"

With a heartfelt bond to our common faith,
Your Martin Niemöller

1. The addressee apparently resided at the Burckhardt house.
2. Niemöller's defamation as an "enemy of the people" was very difficult for him. When he was arrested on July 1, 1937, the official notice read: "Yesterday, the gestapo arrested the Confessing pastor, Martin Niemöller of Berlin-Dahlem, and brought him into court which issued a warrant for his arrest. Niemöller has been making inflammatory statements for some time during his lectures and sermons and has calumniated leading governmental measures in order to alarm the population. Furthermore he has incited resistance against governmental laws and decrees. His statements are part of the permanent content of the foreign press which is hostile to Germany." A newspaper in Bielefeld printed the above notice on the front page under the headline "A Minister of the Devil."

August 24, 1937
To Pastor Wilhelm Niemöller

My beloved brother!

All our plans seem to have been subjected to change; today in any case I heard from Else, who is in Deep, and she will—perhaps—stay there until the 26th, while I had assumed that she would be in Dahlem until Sunday evening. Likewise I have no idea whether you were able to stick with your plan of staying on in Dahlem since the latest note of yours which has reached me is dated August 13. Already there is not much time left until your reserve officer training. Let me know your new address soon.

I have no news to tell; one day is much the same as the other, as would be the case during summer vacation. It's just that the stay here cannot be equated with the latter, even though—like the Apocrypha—"quite good and useful" it may be. Leni is carrying out her duties in Dahlem; she is also mothering Jan, Jutta, and Tini, while Hertha remains with her mother so Else wouldn't have to be so lonely.[1] Sass was ordained last Wednesday and can now take over all my duties, which puts me at ease.[2] Fritz Müller is also back in the country, which is another source of comfort to me![3] This way the church's cast ought to get moving again, and one day even the gentlemen who are our bishops will have to get going again if they value the following of their own pastors and congregation![4] I continue to be in good shape; one good twenty-kilometer march and I'll be alright! I am still receiving many greetings from around the country and the congregation which Else notes down and forwards to me. This love and intercession is of great help; even when the mail stops for a few days I don't miss it. My covenant of peace! My dear boy, give my heartfelt regards to your family. And receive my thanks for all your love and care. We shall continue our office with to-day's word: Isaiah 12:4. With true love and faithfulness.

Your Martin

1. Niemöller's children were Brigitte, Hans Jochen, Heinz Hermann, Jan, Hertha, Jutta, and Tini (Martin). Leni (Helene Bremer) is Else Niemöller's sister.
2. Pastor Wolfgang Sass served the Dahlem congregation for a number of years.
3. Fritz Müller (b. 1889) is the well-known Müller of Dahlem who along with Niemöller played a major role in the growth and struggle of the Confessing church. After the Confessing synod of Oeynhausen, he became chairman of the second provisional leadership group of the German Evangelical church. His brief biographical sketch is in Wilhelm Niemöller, *Lebensbilder aus der Bekennenden Kirche* (Bielefeld, 1949).
4. The bishops referred to are Marahrens, Meiser, and Wurm who continuously impeded the church struggle.

My dear Pauline,

The folks at home tell me that you have happily returned to Frankfurt, and so it seems that I have no choice but to send regular, brief reports there. I could actually do so by using the old phrase "There is nothing new in the East!" because what differentiates one day here from another are really only the very, very small things: the weather, the menu, having slept more or less well, the arrival or nonarrival of the mail, the visit or nonvisit of my attorney! I often think about the time I spent in Poland when I was held up in drydock and had to wait for the submarine to be readied. It was the same feeling: let's not hurry; there'll be another day tomorrow!

In fact I have no news at all to report, neither good nor bad. The mood is animated but not light; instead the old stoicism is coming into its own, along with Ovid's aphorism: *"medio tutissime ibis,"* which someone fairly well translated as "Ibis is safest in the middle." I suppose all your children are gathered around you and the house is never quiet. How I long sometimes for the healthy racket of children! Patience, nothing but patience! At least three children are now at home in Dahlem, and starting tomorrow there'll be four. The older boys are in Tiefenbrunn, Brigitte is in Weimar, mother and Hertha are in Deep, father is in jail. In short, a fine family! Give my regards to your dear Carl, not to mention Martin, Max, Agathe, and Gudula. A special greeting to you, dear Pauline; do pray that I may remain joyous and that I may rejoin my family again. God will grant it!

Faithfully,
Your Martin

August 25, 1937
To Pastor Hans Goethe, Dorf-Güll (Oberhessen) [1]

Dear Colleague!
My wife informs me that you have sent regards; unfortunately I won't receive them personally since I have sacrificed all other mail for that from my family, in order to maintain our contact. Your greetings from the great circle of brethren nevertheless bring such joy and refreshment to my solitude that I thank you truly for your kind thoughtfulness. The weeks drag on; today rounds out the eighth—and so many other brethren are in the same or a similar situation. I can only say that for me this time has passed relatively quickly, and that I have been saved from all despondency. After all, it is not our own affair for which we fight or suffer, stand or fall. Christ our Lord must know how long to let the storm rage. I see demonstrated in the case of my own congregation how the evil men intend to do must, under his guidance, serve the cause of good. Today's word is: "The Lord, your God changed the curse into your blessings, for the Lord your God loves you!" And for this we may gratefully rejoice in faith.

Your Martin Niemöller

1. Pastor Hans Goethe (b. 1906) had been persecuted by the gestapo since 1935. His name was on the church's intercession list; he was prohibited from speaking, from serving as a pastor, and was subject to banishment. He was finally called to the Rimbach congregation in Odenwald where he stayed for sixteen years, retiring in 1971. His story is typical of the persecution which the "younger brethren" suffered.

August 27, 1937
To Pastor Wilhelm Niemöller

My dear Wilhelm!

A fat clutch of mail arrived yesterday, among it cherished greetings from Dahlem on Saturday and Sunday, and the note from Bielefeld on Monday (with the greetings of Mieze[1] and Gabriel[2]). It was a heartfelt joy that you should have preached for me three times, my dear, dear boy! Generally I'm not spoiled by someone doing something for me, especially during this time when you all must surely have enough to do, which I surmise from Gabriel's journey as well. It's delightful to see others—and I *don't* mean *you* now—having to carry out work and responsibility. Let's hope Fritz Müller continues to hold up!

Even with all this uncertainty you'll have to go to your [military] exercises tomorrow! Else was smarter; she is still in Deep, and I'm happy as can be about it. On Wednesday I hope to see her with her cheeks reddened. I have good news from our parents and the boys in Tiefenbrunn as well as from many other people from everywhere, known and unknown. Yesterday there were seventy-six pieces of mail! I'll start a collection! Otherwise, no news; health o.k., weather bad, mood excellent (better than Cadorna, thank God).[3] Wednesday's wonderful selection—Deuteronomy 23:5—is constantly going through my mind these days.* As for the rest, I am patient, read much English at the moment, and am relearning hymns. Don't overdo it on horseback.[4] Our bones are older than they were in 1917, or 1920 for that matter! May God protect every

---

*"The Lord your God refused to listen to Balaam and turned his denunciation into a blessing, because the Lord your God loved you."

seaman and horseman, as well as some of the gentlemen in the infantry! Farewell! My innermost thoughts are with you! Always,

Your Martin

1. Mieze is Mrs. Maria Opitz, one of the Niemöller sisters.
2. Gabriel refers to Pastor Walter Gabriel from Halle/Saale who went with Wilhelm Niemöller to the fifth Confessing synod of the Old Prussian Union in Lippstadt on August 23. The synod was held from August 21 to 27 under the chairmanship of Pastor Karl Lücking.
3. This reference is to the battle for the Ruhr during World War I. Cadorna, chief of the Italian general staff, lost the battle of Karfreit and was reputed to have always been in a bad mood.
4. Wilhelm Niemöller was called up for an exercise of the Sixth Artillery Regiment on August 28 at the request of Major Köhler. Köhler's friendship did not protect him from further interference by the gestapo (interrogation, loss of passport, etc.).

August 28, 1937
To Unknown[1]

Dear Brother!

I've been waiting to send you a note for some time but I did not know if you were still in the hospital. Now I gather from one of Wilhelm's postcards that you were still there as of a week ago, and so I am trying my luck because today's selection—"Your right hand holds me"—turned my first thoughts to you. God grant your complete recuperation so that the both of us who are now out of action may once again work with the brethren. Like Aaron and Hur in the Amalekite battle, we also have our duty and it should suffice until we are called to another!

About myself I can tell you—God be thanked—only good news: I lack nothing for body, soul, and spirit. After my first flare-up over this disgrace cooled down, I got my sense of humor back: "Let them mock, let them laugh, Lord my Savior. . . ." I am furthermore in the agreeable position of having everything go well at home, with my dear wife finally beginning to be cheerful again. That was my only worry, and he has made everything well! I gather from quite a few notes that the brethren in the country have become quite brave. We do live, after all, in 1937. Already we can look back over the visible traces of four years, and we don't want to cease being thankful for that. At this point, we "old fighters" may already step into the background a little bit (where we may join God's lectures for the select)! Remember me to your dear wife; may our Lord Jesus Christ grant you renewed confidence, strength, and joy daily, and a firm and happy heart! With old, brotherly love

Your Martin Niemöller

1. The addressee is quite certainly Pastor Karl Immer (b. 1888) of Barmen-Gemarke, the father of the Confessing synods. He was arrested on August 5, 1937, and brought to Berlin where he suffered a stroke in the Alexanderplatz prison.

... I am returning your greetings most sincerely from this year's involuntary summer home where my overly lengthy stay—two months to date—nevertheless agrees well with me! For some time now I have not been enjoying it, but then I have not been asked to either! Jokes aside, it is kind of you to think of me! There is so much mail that I am never finished thanking everyone, and that's a good thing too because otherwise there is nothing to do, and it's senseless to occupy myself with the trial so long as there is no date in sight. There are strange circumstances, to be sure. The British did not manage to catch me, although they wanted to, and now someone had to do it who did not actually want to, as he has let me know.[2] Perhaps I could write a story about it later which could be included in *Toller Bomberg*.

My life moves along quite leisurely, and still I am astonished how the days and weeks vanish; it's just that one becomes older and unlearns the beautiful art of being bored. I'm generally not impatient, but I always think that the real Protestant church ought to open its mouth so wide that it could be heard from Dan to Beersheba. Well, it will happen. Else and the children—praise God—are well, just as there are all sorts of reasons to be thankful and to look confidently to the future. There is only one to whom is given all power. Regards to your children and to T.[3]

In old affection,
Your Martin

1. The addressee of this postcard, of which there is only a handwritten copy, is apparently Dr. Robert Schmitt, a pharmacist from Hamm who married a cousin of the Niemöllers, Grete.
2. Apparently a reference to Dr. Franz Gürtner.
3. T. is presumed to be the church superintendent in Hamm, Arnold Torhorst, who always showed a faithful concern for Niemöller.

August 30, 1937
To Superintendent Arnold Torhorst, Hamm

Dear Mr. Superintendent,
The note you intended for me was received by my wife who informed me of it. At least I am able to thank you without an intermediary! I've been sitting here for almost nine weeks now, and that is a fairly boring business in itself even if I did not do anything else. But fortunately I have not been thrown into a dark medieval dungeon, even though my view is restricted to a small piece of blue or overcast sky! And I don't have to subsist on bread and water, which still would be better than nothing, though I would rather eat my wife's cooking. And I don't have to sap my failing strength with forced labor, although given my old bones, scrubbing my cell on hands and knees is not the pure joy with which I would call down the blessings of heaven upon those who brought me here!
But taking everything as a whole, I feel fine, I am happy, rejoicing and noticing that these weeks have not diminished my faith, not to mention the manifold and ample love which greets and carries me on all sides! And the hope lives that this whole situation will not last one second longer than our heavenly father deems good and necessary. That I still had to and have to learn a good bit of patience, I'll gladly confess. Meanwhile, everything continues on the outside; the church lives and our Lord Jesus Christ is with her and will carry on in the spirit of today's selection: Zechariah 9:16.* My regards to your dear wife and the young ones, as well as to the brethren everywhere.

Sincerely,
Your Martin Niemöller

*"So on that day the Lord their God will save them, his own people, like sheep, setting them all about his land, like jewels set to sparkle in a crown."

August 31, 1937
To Pastor Wilhelm Niemöller

Dear Wilhelm,

It won't do for me to let today pass without sending you a note. It is forbidden both by the selection and the textbook! So our brotherly love shall remain steadfast. Were you too in Lippstadt? Today I received a postcard from there, from Niesel,[1] Müller, and Vogel;[2] it reported news of the synod.[3] And when I was questioned a little while ago (it's starting again, God be thanked) I learned that my state attorney was there at the same time![4] Tableau!

Last night Else was supposed to have returned from Deep and I'm expecting her during visiting hours tomorrow morning. This time I'm looking forward to it because I'm under the impression that she has really recuperated and should be able to withstand—physically also—the coming gusts. So far as I'm concerned I'm well armed, although I haven't touched the files for my trial for almost three weeks. After a while it just becomes too distasteful. On the other hand, Else indicated to me that things were going well for the Confessing church and that the bishops were attempting to stand their ground.[5] Whatever heals itself is a good thing. Niesel writes that he is going on vacation. These lucky people! I won't complain, however, even though I'm not losing my rancor because of my lost vacation. You are not any better off either! How is the Prussian drill? Are your bones going along—and how about the appendix? So, my dear brother! Be well; may God grant us a happy reunion: "Whoever lies in God's lap will remain happy in all misfortune" Give my regards to the beautiful city! With love and faith,

Your Martin

1. Pastor Wilhelm Niesel (b. 1903) was, like Martin Niemöller, a member of the counsel of the Evangelical church of the Old Prussian Union, whose head was Friedrich Müller of Dahlem.

2. Pastor Heinrich Vogel (b. 1902) from Dobbrikow was one of the "early fighters" of the Confessing church who was noted in the Confessing synods for his presentations and reports.

3. The fifth Confessing synod (August 21–27, 1937) was, for the first time, led by Pastor Lücking of Dortmund rather than by Karl Koch. Its dissolution was anticipated each day because it concerned itself with the "church struggle resolutions" of the Prussian Council of Brethren, with which the synod was in complete accord. These resolutions called for abstention from the church elections planned by Hitler, ageed to the custom of announcing during church services the names of those who had renounced church membership, and seriously addressed the issue of governmental interference in the financial matters of the church. Strangely enough, the synod ended without having been disrupted by the authorities.

4. The interrogation session concerned Martin Niemöller's sermon of June 17 and was conducted by state attorney Görisch. Subsequent interrogations on September 2, 3, and 9 concerned sermons preached by Niemöller on May 25 in Lichterfelde, June 8 in Lankwitz, June 14 in Dahlem, and June 18 in Bielefeld; and on September 9 and November 11, 1936, in Bielefeld and Gütersloh, respectively.

5. During this period, much confidence was placed in the three "intact" bishops who belonged to the Kassel group, created on July 6, 1937. This group had been able to unite the actions of the Conference of Bishops, the provisional leadership of the German Evangelical church, and the Council of the German Evangelical Lutheran church. This effort fell apart completely the following year.

(Undated)
To Pastor Gerber, Wiesbaden[1]

Dear Brother Gerber,
Your dear greetings—among the many which bear witness to the intercession and the sharing of the load by the congregation for the brethren who are under arrest—have reached me. If we become a church that hears and prays during this time of difficulty, then it's won, no matter what else breaks down. During these days, I've read something by Bezzel: "We'll be happy and free again only after we have experienced hate because of our Christian belief."[2] That is happening now, and thus with God's grace it will be along the lines of Hebrews 12:11.* With deep thanks and heartfelt regards.

Your Martin Niemöller

*"Discipline, no doubt, is never pleasant. At the time it seems painful, but in the end it yields for those who have been trained by it the peaceful harvest of an honest life."

1. Pastor Dr. Hermann Gerber (b. 1910) was assistant pastor in Heppenheim and was taken into protective custody there. He was subsequently removed by Bishop Dietrich and until the war was manager of the parsonage in Wörrstadt. Later he served pastorates in Altweilnau and Königstein and became head of the United Church Pastors' Office for Radio and Television in Darmstadt.
2. Dr. Hermann Bezzel (1861–1917) was rector of the Deaconess Institute in Neuendettelsau, later president of the Protestant Upper Consistory in Munich.

October 14, 1937
To Miss Hermine Hermes

Dear Miss Hermes!
It is kind of you to let me participate a bit in what's taking place via your card of September 9. According to the paper, it looks as though the church these days consisted solely of music and 12,000 Thuringians. But—thank God—there are still the 7,000 of 1 Kings 19:18, and what applies to the people of the promised land is written and said in 2 Kings 6:16.[1] Let's stay with it—with joy! Sincerely and in faith, and thanks also for your greetings of October 9.

Your Martin Niemöller

1. The Thuringian wing of the German Christians was considered to be a radical group. In 1937 it had much room to maneuver and was able to put out quite a bit of propaganda in the political and religious press. In the first biblical passage cited, reference is made to the 7,000 Israelites who "have not bent the knee to Baal." The second passage reads: "Do not be afraid, for those who are on our side are more than those on theirs." Citation of these two biblical passages was seen at the time as "endangering the State."

October 17, 1937
To Unknown

. . . Your greetings have gladdened me in my solitude and I want to convey my heartfelt thanks.[1] The promise of today's selection gives, in advance, the lie to all our worries: "I shall give my people a place and I shall plant them that they may dwell in a place of their own, and move no more, neither shall the children of wickedness afflict them anymore, as before." He remains faithful! . . .

1. On October 15 during a meeting of the Pastors' Emergency League in Berlin, it was formally determined that Martin Niemöller should remain as head of the league. Two days earlier, the district attorney had again visited Niemöller in person to determine what remarks he had made concerning the church elections which had been ordered and announced by Hitler on February 15, 1937. Niemöller could only report that the Prussian Council of Brethren had rejected participation in such elections and that the Confessing synod of Lippstadt had endorsed that position.

October 23, 1937
To Jutta Niemöller[1]

My dear Jutta!
I do have to write to tell you how very proud I am of you! Your mother told me yesterday that you'll be the only one of your class who will "jump a grade." I would not allow it—I believe—were it not for the fact that this way you will be with Hertha. Both of you must surely be very happy about this?! The picture that Dr. L. took of both you and your mother is always in front of me. My love to you and Hertha.

Your faithful Dad

1. Jutta, almost nine years old at the time, was a physically weak child. She died quite suddenly on December 30, 1944, in Starnberg.

October 24, 1937
To Mrs. Else Niemöller

My Beloved Else!

Now it's Sunday once again, the seventeenth in this circle of weeks; I've just returned from "church" and my thoughts are turning to you and to Wilhelm, who is now still standing in my pulpit. I hope you will tell me about the service; the attendance I hope is not suffering from the weather. I am so calm, happy, and thankful in the knowledge that Wilhelm is taking care of the congregation: Philippians 2:20.* Here, we heard a sermon by Pastor Klatt[1] on a passage from John 4:21–34. The sermon was decent, but what a sad thing the singing was, if one gets to comparing! Earlier our exercise hour was considerably foreshortened by heavy rain, and for the first time I was happy to have my raincoat.

Is it possible that today—something I would hope—you can have a quiet afternoon at home before Brigitte's departure? In any event, I'll think of you faithfully. The mail arrived again yesterday at noon; now I have your cards of the 20th and 22d, as well as the note of the 21st from the new Kranzler. I have Fritz's letter as well;[2] he ought to calm down—he knows that I don't have corns. But I would like to know if he stayed at the Elephant Hotel in Weimar, and whether he saw Brigitte there. That Fritz should really have worried about Tini lately has given me quite a jolt! You don't have any reason to worry about me; I'm sure this fainting won't repeat itself. On the other hand, you'll have to learn to accept the fact that I'm slowly losing my slender waistline; yesterday I had to resew a button on my vest. Who knows what a fat, well-padded hide is good for. Perhaps a layer of fat helps one to endure one's

*"There is no one else here who sees things as I do, and takes a genuine interest in your concerns."

longings?! But at least we were able to see one another and talk, and I'm under the impression that the time is passing more quickly every day. A week from tomorrow, our time will already come again! If possible, bring Wilhelm and Fritz along, and the time after that—please—bring Tini!

By the way, you did not respond at all to my raising the question of Christmas, but I'd like to think about it and prepare for it with you! And you shouldn't—especially at this time—calculate so cautiously! The cost of my trial I have mentally passed along to the church council; how to do it is still my patent and my secret. True, the lawyers will have to have a payment on the account soon. I hope they have not come to you with this; from my view of things, the time has already come because all three have had considerable expenses.[3] Please do speak with Miss Hermes about this and get it moving; otherwise this notion will begin to bother me! And what about Wilhelm's travel expenses which must be already in the hundreds?

Among yesterday's mail, in addition to two more cards from the Burckhardt house, there was a note from Immer from Sauerland. I'm afraid he is in a bad situation and I would like to know more details.[4] Do ask Niesel about it sometime! Some of the latest notes sound a little discouraged (for example, Gollwitzer);[5] I'm afraid this can be traced back to the article in *German Justice.*[6] That should not be taken too seriously; instead it should be answered *firmly* and unequivocally by the church, or under certain circumstances, answered in front of the congregation. But there should be no discussion, neither with the so called "church council" nor with Dr. Gürtner.[7] The church has its foundation in its confession, and its constitution is based on that; and everything that has happened and has been done to deny the former and to injure the latter is completely beyond the scope of any possible discussion, i.e., negotiation. I am quite calm and confident in my conviction that any replay of the events of 1933–34, on the basis of an alleged better "legal foundation" must fail.[8] Furthermore, the last word is spoken by the Lord of the Church! Excuse the "diversion" but do tell those whose business it is!

Something completely different: You gave me a few addresses but unfortunately they are absolutely insufficient. Bibra has returned to Nürnberg—and I'd like to know his address *there.* Kehrl in Kolberg:[9] I have the address; I'd like to know whether he is a *pastor.* Kuhlchen can look that up in *Evangelical Germany.* I'm also enclosing two cards whose signatures will have to be taken care of in the same way. And since I'm at it, I'm supposed to send you regards from Miss Helga Rusche (a theological student formerly in Berlin, now in Marburg). So that completes my official requests and chores, now I want to take a nap; more this afternoon!

2:30 P.M.

My short luncheon nap—today a success by the way—is over, while I assume at this hour that you are still resting in the arm of Morpheus, tired by church, Sunday school, and the big family supper. I just read Neugebauer's article on "Tradition and the Present" in the *Deutsche Allgemeine Zeitung;* my other reading of German novels is a questionable joy— either a "Decline of the West" mood or "Hurrah, we are still alive and just getting started!" On the other hand, you'll be interested that I've been enthusiastically reading Macaulay's *History of England* for several days. To discover such a treasure you first have to sit in the brig for three and a half months! I am now at Cromwell and am amazed by the superior intelligence and level-headed presentation of a historian who is completely involved but nevertheless passionately avoids passing judgment. I still have one delectable week ahead of me with these two volumes—if the lawyers leave me alone. But since they believe in a court date as little as I do, they probably won't show too often! I have reached a dead-point with the hymnal—my memory goes on strike when it is supposed to learn; so instead I sing a few hymns in the evenings. I'm almost through the New Testament (in Greek) for the second time. At the moment I am reading the letter to the Hebrews.

Now, one more question! All kinds of people are writing to me about my picture with three lines (with quotation) written underneath, which they supposedly have.[10] What actually is it, and can you get me a copy; I would like to know if that is really my writing! Especially since I don't know of any *dicta probantia******* which I might have authored! Will Hertha and

**"approved sayings"

Jutta be already attending Gertrud School starting next Easter? Thank God we still have the little one to go. He is growing up so fast, Jochen has almost frightened me! Please do tell him that I expect him to be your right hand and support; are his violin lessons starting up again already? Is he still convinced he wants to become a theologian? Enough questions, even though I would like to continue about Brigitte, Hermann, Jan, and all the friends. And I would like to know a few things concerning you and the congregation. Next time! My general disposition is quite good and I can only hope that everyone sleeps as soundly as I do, "excepting these bonds" (Acts 26:29). Should there be quiet times again, I'll take a year's vacation and write down for our children and their children the experiences from 1931 till now. But when will that time be? "Gird your soul with patience!" I am happy as long as you are alright and when I hear that the brethren are standing fast! My deepest love to you and the whole house, my dear, dear Else!

In faith always,
Your Martin

1. Pastor Detloff Klatt (b. 1882) was pastor of the prison at Moabit. Later, he wrote the book *Treffpunkt Berlin-Moabit* (Berlin, no date).

2. Fritz is Mrs. Niemöller's brother, Dr. Friedrich Bremer, medical director of the Elizabeth Hospital in Berlin.

3. Three attorneys were, at this point, working on Niemöller's behalf: Dr. Horst Holstein, Dr. Willy Hahn, and attorney Hans Koch, who was executed on April 24, 1945, for his participation in the plot against Hitler's life.

4. Pastor Karl Immer had to recuperate for a lengthy period after his release from jail.

5. Pastor Helmut Gollwitzer (b. 1910) was at the center of work in the Dahlem congregation after Niemöller's arrest.

6. *Deutsche Justiz (German Justice)* was edited by Dr. Franz Gürtner. Following a court ruling, an announcement was published on September 11, 1937, to the effect that the recognition of all groups of the German Evangelical church could not be derived from the decree of the reichschancellor on February 15, 1937, concerning the convocation of a general synod for the purpose of creating a constitution. His announcement read: "The German Evangelical church as a Christian corporation under civil law can be comprised only of members and groups who recognize the church regime as appointed by the Führer or delegated to the reichsminister for church affairs, not those which have split off, have created their

own organs, and one disputing the legality of the church regime authorized by the state. The Confessing church belongs to this latter group; it is no longer a part of the German Evangelical church under civil law but an independent group standing alongside the German Evangelical church which is therefore not entitled to the rights of a religious corporation recognized by the state under civil law."

7. Dr. Franz Gürtner (b. 1881) was reichsminister for justice and personally was quite well disposed toward Niemöller.

8. The pessimistic mood of the Confessing church was created during this period by a decree of the S.S. reichsführer which strictly forbade the teaching and ordination practices of the Confessing church.

9. Student leader Rudolf Kehrl was an energetic collaborator of the Confessing church in Pomerania. He lived in Kolberg and after the war worked for the church in Jena.

10. The picture about which Niemöller inquires shows him in civilian clothes and was taken from his book, *Vom U-Boot zur Kanzel* (*From U-boat to Pulpit*). Underneath the picture is a quote from one of his sermons: "We do not need to ask how much faith we have in ourselves, but we will be asked if we have faith in God's word, that God's word is and does what it says!" The first printing, ordered by Heinrich Held in Essen and printed by Schmiedke Printers in Mühlheim, numbered 150,000 copies, and another edition by another printer ran 100,000 copies. That a sample went in and out of cell 448 in Moabit is one of the amusing incidents with which the church struggle was richly endowed.

October 25, 1937
To Mrs. Else Niemöller

My dearest!
Next, I'll cease all correspondence with you. First my lawyer asks me if I am in financial difficulty; there is supposed to be talk that I can't afford the better sort of daily bread here anymore; then I get a postcard from Asmussen who is worried about my health. It appears to me that you should take Mr. Ohnesorge's[1] lecture a little more to heart and ensure the privacy of the mails, i.e., you should not let my letters lie about! Otherwise you'll suddenly be receiving letters of condolence. Here is another reprimand: for the first time in weeks the mail came today (seventeen pieces) without including a single one from you or anyone in the house. But I'll take that as a good sign! Mrs. Schmitt wrote nicely of Hermann which was balm for the father in me! I'm just afraid that the boy will be silent toward us, now that Jochen is not with him anymore.

I survived last Sunday in fine fettle and was very pleased with Holstein's visit this morning.[2] You ought to give my very special regards to Schako.[3] "Faithfulness is no empty delusion." Did Wilhelm come and preach? Asmussen, Müller, and Böhm[4] wrote while they were on the tram; Müller is apparently going to see his wife again.[5] Fritz's letter was a real feast for me; once I'm back home again he should drive us for three days to Naumburg, Weimar, and Eisenach to refresh our friendship and dear memories. The day is so beautiful again that my thoughts are turning to travel! This week will now complete the fourth month: *hora ruit*!* Is Tini alright again? I think a lot about him but also about all of you! The whole thing is still like a dream to me. "The brief questioning" to

*"The hour hastens."

60

which I was ostensibly taken is beginning to be lengthy; one simply is not quite familiar yet with the new terminology! Be that as it may, "Your heavenly father has advice in all matters!" Luke 22:35** I think of you with true love, my dear. Love and kisses,

Your Martin

**The quotation could be Niemöller's interpretation of the biblical passage cited: "He said to them, 'when I sent you out barefoot without purse or pack, were you ever short of anything?' " Or perhaps it is a reference to Matthew 6:32: "because your heavenly Father knows that you need them all."

1. This mention of the chief of the Reich postal ministry, Dr. Wilhelm Ohnesorge, appears to point to the constant invasion of the privacy of the mails.
2. Dr. Horst Holstein, Niemöller's attorney.
3. Captain Conrad Schako who was active in the work of the Scripture Circle and who would show up at events of the Confessing church wearing his uniform.
4. Pastor Hans Böhm who, after 1936, belonged to the provisional leadership of the Confessing church, along with Müller, Albertz, Forck, Fricke, and Dr. Günther, a regional court official.
5. Pastor Müller was en route to see his ill wife.

October 27, 1937
To Mrs. Else Niemöller

My beloved Else!

It seems that once again the time for the Sunday letter has arrived, and this time it will sound totally happy because just a little while ago I received among thirty-one pieces of mail both your postcards from Sunday and Monday, which removed the anguish I felt in my heart yesterday. From your description of the Sunday supper with five children at the table, I surmise that Jan's flu was of a fairly sporadic nature. Hertha's little letter is so dear that I have already read it three or four times. And that counts for even more since at the moment I can hardly work through my mail. So that I won't forget, one of the cards signed by Müller, Böhm, Thadden, etc. was also cosigned by a Mr. Butler (?). I laughed out loud over the headline in the *Deutsche Allgemeine Zeitung*: "Rudolph Hess on the Way to Rome." In the latter case, it is hard not to believe in malice! I hope good old Silex[1] won't get in trouble for it! These "pilgrims to Rome" are quite something anyway.[2]

But the reason I am so happy and have begun the day with "Praise the Lord, all who honor him" is the great consolation that Wilhelm will take over the care of the congregation. There were already some echoes in the mail today; now I can sleep in peace again; God only grant that he remains in good health and that his strength is sufficient! I think of Emmchen[3] in Lippstadt: "Drive carefully, you're chauffeuring nothing but Niemöllers!" Who will mark our graves! . . .[4] But seriously, do take good care of him and take care that he doesn't take on too much. I'm doubly thankful to him in view of Ingeborg who'll miss him very much! And how about you, darling? If you can't get to sleep and red wine won't help, do give beer a try like my Uncle Fritz in Emden did. Until now I'd always been under the impression that from ten o'clock on you had as little trouble getting to sleep as the effort was great to stay awake! *Tempora mutantur!* . . .* But as compensation I'm better at it, only at noon it doesn't want to come on with its usual promptness. But that is easily explained by the fact that I sleep eight hours—almost regularly—without interruption.

At the moment, my attorneys are quite touching: Monday morning Holstein was here, yesterday Koch, today Hahn. But I had to console all three of them; they must suffer more from the barred doors than I do. Today, Hahn really perked up a little when I told him that I regarded this whole development in a very positive light for the Evangelical church. Yesterday I read that Dr. Gürtner had an automobile accident and is slightly injured. If I were at home I'd visit him in the hospital, but from what I hear it's not serious! Which reminds me that the sisters have written me that Grandmother Tietz has become a bit shaky; could you take her a Tokay or some such thing in my name sometime? Who got the idea to present you with a handmade nightgown? That's really something! I have to echo my old first officer of the *Thüringen*. The other old ditty from days of old fits in fairly well also: "It's lovely aboard a submarine/And there are things to do/Whereof those on a battleship/Haven't got a clue," since it belongs in the realm of the Tenth Muse. Christa Müller sent me the pleasant Morgenstern poem about the reading glasses which pulls the text together.[5] Well, you know it, and by the Tenth Muse I don't mean Christa M.! Enough of the cruel games, but it all stems from that nightgown!

With the passing of today we are already crossing the summit again; only four days until we see each other again on Monday! By now I've been here as long as my trip in U-151 lasted; only this time I have not sunk 50,000 tons! Still, it cannot have been completely wasted. I just hope that I won't have to serve out the rest of my navy career over again in this place. A colleague with a kind heart expressed to me his sorrow that I should be kicked out of the third profession I had

*"Times change."

63

come to love. But given his emeritus status, he's entitled to extenuating circumstances! At first work is no doubt going to be somewhat difficult, and otherwise I feel that I am still right in the thick of my profession, despite everything, and I'm especially looking forward to the young people, just as I am often pleased with the young people in my view from here. It's good that the evenings for the confirmed youth are going again! There is quite a bit happening among the students, and the young theologians are really refreshing! Hermann has written to me from Tiefenbrunn after all, and quite nicely at that; I understand he's keeping a diary—I'd sure like to take a look inside. Feelings assuredly play no role there, but chamois, stags, deer, birds, snow, and mountains do! You may tell Jochen that with his reference to Hebrews 12 he spoke both from the heart and to my heart. There is where a portion of father Bremer's inheritance comes through; I would not have been able to write a letter like that to my father when I was fifteen years old. But despite the sprained finger, the handwriting is so terrible that I'd have to take recourse to the vocabulary of my old sergeant in the First Sea Battalion in order to grade it properly. I also refuse all paternal responsibility for this "inheritance"; it must come from the Borbergs or the Frielinghauses. I wonder how it went yesterday at Landois (the doctor) with Tini? Does the boy still behave as well? For his recuperation, a greeting from mother; in his "greetings from father" I'd like to give him a hearty kiss. But those are the grapes which, for the moment, are still hanging too high. Of the pictures you sent, I like the one quite well where you are laughing—somewhat restrained and through a veil—Hertha is looking ahead so that one can't see her eyes, but Jutta is quite delightful with her pensive child's gaze. Mrs. Schmitt wrote that we must be quite happy about our children.[6] One could also agree with Hermann: "so much racket!" But from a distance I do agree with Mrs. Schmitt. Faithful Sass reports almost daily and keeps me well informed; does Eisenhardt still come around occasionally?[7] Or is he completely occupied with his preparations for the exam? I have written a card to Mrs. R.[8] and to Sells and Mrs. Pietschker.

Evening nears and the sun is setting. It was a beautiful day, within and without. Farewell, dear heart; I am looking forward to Monday and beyond that "lo the day" which will surely dawn. How will I be able to manage all my things then? You'll have to arrange for a suitcase and a car! But I'm sure it will be a while yet, and so be it. Meanwhile, let's not forget today's selection: Psalm 71:15.** With deep love,

Your Martin

**"All day long thy righteousness, thy saving acts, shall be upon my lips."

1. Karl Heinrich Silex (b. 1896), a former navy officer, was from 1933 to 1943 editor-in-chief of the *Deutsche Allgemeine Zeitung*.
2. A possible reference to Alfred Rosenberg's *Protestant Pilgrims to Rome* (1935). Rosenberg was also author of *The Betrayal of Luther* and the infamous *Myth of the Twentieth Century*.
3. Emma Bolhöfer was a cousin of the Niemöllers who lived in Lippstadt.
4. A quotation from the poems of Börries von Münchhausen: "Wer soll unsre Runen ritzen, wenn wir es nicht selber tun?"
5. Christa Müller was a curate in Dahlem.
6. Mrs. Schmitt was the wife of the reichsminister for economics, Kurt Schmitt, who held office from 1933 to 1935. Both took a friendly interest in the Niemöller family.
7. Ernst Eisenhardt (b. 1909) was from Berlin and began his activity in the church struggle as a volunteer in Dahlem on May 11, 1933. He was prepared to do any job: he went to Ulm in Martin Niemöller's place to put the latter's signature on the Ulm Declaration, was arrested frequently, helped untiringly with the preparations for Niemöller's trial, was ordained September 7, 1938, by Hans Asmussen, having completed his exams illegally, and was an illegal pastor of the Confessing church in Mark Brandenburg. After the war, he was a pastor in Ickern (Westphalia) and superintendent of the church district in Herne. He died in 1970.
8. "Mrs. R." is Mrs. Olga Rigele, Hermann Göring's sister, who was well disposed toward the Confessing church.

October 28, 1937
Mrs. Else Niemöller

Dearest Wife!
Today was restless but beautiful. First thing this morning assessor Vogel arrived, followed by his boss Holstein from whom I learned that he received a certificate of good conduct for me from Hassell.[1] He also received a letter from General Salmuth![2] But the highlight came when I was called into court during lunch and there met Günter Deutecom whom I had confirmed, and who had managed with iron tenacity to see and talk to me![3] A touching young man, and the court was kind enough to let this conversation take place in the justice building, so that we were able to talk quite peacefully for almost an hour! Günter D. was in Passau for his labor service and will be going to Reichenhall for his military service. He had much on his mind because of the battle against the church faith; it was interesting and frightening at the same time! But he is holding up fine.

Well, that was *the* event today. There was no mail, but after yesterday's blessing I suppose I can do without for one day. Instead, I read Kerrl's letter to Wurm in the paper.[4] That could and probably ought to be a parallel to my case; I don't believe Wurm will back out. But the doctoral examination question is being asked as to whether Kerrl has the right to interfere in internal church matters and to withdraw himself from all criticism, simply by virtue of his public office. Perhaps this incident will get the dammed up river flowing again. That will be alright by me. But if it should not happen, I won't be disheartened! I'm a completely changed person since I know Wilhelm is at your side; now, I believe, I could stand it for years; now I'm not even scared by the letter of Zimmerman and company which you mentioned a while ago! And now we are only separated by three days and four nights until we see one another again on Monday; I hope you'll bring fresh, good news of all our seven! This time I'd like to ask you to give my special regard to the Schaetzel circle,[5] but also of course our whole household, Wilhelm and the five children who now surround you. I do love you *sooo* much. Do read the proverb sometime which someone told me today: Proverbs 14:26.* And please do me a favor and go easy on yourself; you don't have to worry about me—I'm doing *well.* With all my heart and faith,

Your Martin

*"A strong man who trusts in the fear of the Lord will be a refuge for his sons."

1. Hassell is Ulrich von Hassell (b. 1881) who was ambassador to Rome from 1932 to 1937 and was executed in September 1944 as one of the participants in the plot against Hitler.
2. Major General Freiherr von Salmuth gave the clearest testimony on Niemöller's behalf; it included a sharp attack on the accusers "Along with millions of Germans," he wrote, "I sharply condemn such an imputation."
3. Günter Deutecom continued to write to Niemöller from the battlefield after Niemöller had been sent to the concentration camp.
4. Because the church council of Württemberg had condemned the methods of Bishop Melle and his conduct during the ecumenical conference at Oxford, Hans Kerrl, the reichsminister for church affairs, wrote an open letter to Bishop Wurm in the *Flammenzeichen,* accusing him of treason. Wurm gave an appropriate answer in a personal letter, avoiding turning the matter into a public dispute.
5. The Schaetzel circle was a Bible study group which met in the house of Oberregierungsrat Schaetzel in Dahlem.

November 1, 1937
To Mrs. Else Niemöller

My darling!

I was so very happy about today's reunion—it was so nice and unburdened—just as I had hoped.[1] If only you looked healthier!! Wouldn't you perhaps like to go to Rose's for a few days after all?[2] Each time, I'm under the impression that you are smaller and thinner, and that must not be. The main obstacle is still ahead of us! The files, I hear, are once again at the minister's; furthermore, I was just questioned once again! It's back and forth. If Fritz should talk again with Dr. Gürtner (which in my view can't hurt) he should not refer to me; I would like to keep my hands free and don't want to be given any personal consideration! Meanwhile the attorney (K.)[3] has been here as well; he was apparently somewhat favorably impressed with my plan of my writing a letter to G.[4] But we'll wait out this week. Other than that I don't see any possibility of doing something.

So the car is going to be bought and named "Katharina von Boza"; let's hope we'll be able to use it in the not too distant future. After your departure it weighed heavily on my mind that I did not ask about Ingeborg who was not feeling well last week. Wilhelm was badly slighted in general, but you must tell him how much I enjoyed it! That was a stupid thing yesterday, and since then I've been reproaching myself with Brigitte's confirmation passage: "It is a marvellous thing that happens by grace: the heart becomes firm." Luther was quite a judge of human nature when he translated Jeremiah 17:9: "an obstinate and disheartening thing." But today the barometer is rising again.

Should my trial start now, it will drag out over Christmas and the New Year, of all times! But we'll look at it positively, my dear! "Behold, what love. . . ."* And now give my regards to everyone at home! I am very happy today even though I am not making jokes. How is it with the finances for Wilhelm? Well, I'm sure you'll still answer some of the questions in my letters?! More tomorrow! Heartfelt kisses from

Your Martin

*Apparent reference to 1 John 3:1: "How great is the love that the Father has shown to us! We were called God's children, and such we are."

1. On her visit of November 1, Else Niemöller was accompanied by her brother, Professor Dr. Fritz Bremer, and by Wilhelm Niemöller.
2. Rose is Else's friend, Mrs. Rose Matz, the wife of the archeologist Professor Dr. Friedrich Matz of Münster.
3. Dr. Hans Koch.
4. It is unclear whether this reference is to Hermann Göring or to reichsminister for justice Dr. Gürtner. To whomever intended, there is no record that a letter was ever sent.

November 2, 1937
To Mrs. Else Niemöller

Dearest Wife!

This time you won't be getting a Sunday letter, so don't wait for it in vain. Instead, I'll write to you at greater length tomorrow! Today, I received Friday's letter and was very happy about it; it was like a heady wine for me! I hope you regained your composure quickly yesterday; it was a small drop of bitterness at the joy of our reunion. But you really don't have to worry about me so much, and you'll make my situation easier if you remember that I am doing as well or better than we have any right to expect. I assume Fritz and Wilhelm dried your tears quickly! We'll just have to have some more patience, and the time will come when these months will appear as one short day. I am already looking forward to the 11th; at that time we'll be able to look a little further into the future. If the thought of Christmas is giving you trouble, just leave the preparations be. Should I get out earlier, together we'll make up quickly whatever is missing. And if not, you can send the kids on vacation, should that be necessary.

Both Jochen and Jan should take to heart Luke's word (16:10);* I mean their handwriting, otherwise I enjoy their comments. Right up there with Putz's[1] letter is today's letter from Wehrhahn[2] which is really something special. And you have to tell Wilhelm that my thoughts are with him and concern him! And now farewell, my darling; give my love to the household, especially the children. Yesterday I wrote another card to Brigitte. Both of us will want to hold the passage in Hebrews 12:3** before our mind's eye, as well as the beautiful verse of Luther's which was given me from several sources in

*"The man who can be trusted in little things can be trusted also in great; and the man who is dishonest in little things is dishonest also in great things."

**"Think of him that submitted to such opposition from sinners: that will help you not to lose heart and grow faint."

the past few days: "And whether it lasts through the night, and once again till dawn. . . ." With faith and strongest love,

Your Martin

1. Eduard Putz (b. 1907) was pastor in Fürth. Niemöller was able to return the favor when, after the war, he testified on Putz's behalf during the denazification hearings.
2. Dr. Herbert Wehrhahn was an active member of the Dahlem congregation and friend of the Niemöllers who gave valuable service during the trial. After the war, he became a professor at Saarbrücken.

November 3, 1937
To an Imprisoned Colleague

. . . Slowly—step by step—I am following your tracks, and step by step I am learning what you learned: that the Lord who *has* done great things for us does not tire of continuing to do great things for us. And thus it rings forth again and again from our hearts: "We are glad for it!" I am happy for you and your wife that you are now refreshed. May our Lord and Master continue to be with you and with us. . . .

My dearest Elslein!

It is eleven o'clock in the morning, but since the mail just arrived and brought your card of Sunday, I don't want to wait until the afternoon to write. Holstein was here on a short visit a while ago and I had to talk with him about my latest questioning. He said you were worried about me: apparently we are making life difficult for one another because of our love! I'm really well when I know you are happy and in possession of your strength. Naturally, one always has to fight one's battle with impatience, and it would be terrible if I didn't *want* to be home! But in that regard, I just do whatever has to be done each day, and the rest we'll leave to Christ our Lord. At the moment, the attorneys can't work on anything other than what has already been started. Let's just wait! We'll see one another again a week from tomorrow—if we're alive and God willing—I'm already looking forward to it.

Today I received thirty-nine pieces of mail again, and I'll wait and read them over in the course of the day. I did notice to my surprise and joy a long letter from Seelmann-Eggebert.[1] I am really quite happy and thankful—come what may in the future—knowing that all of you are quite well taken care of and supported by the love of the Dahlem congregation. There is a fine interpretation in the Luther devotion for today of Proverbs 10:28: "The wail of the righteous will turn to joy!" By the way, Bunke from Oberstdorf wrote,[2] and so did Mrs. Wrede; and how touching the good Mrs. Wieligmann is! The brethren around the country assure me again and again that my "imprisonment" is not without purpose. But without the dialectic of the gospel, I could not gain clarity—in this regard. God drives his handiwork forward by suspending his most active people. That goes along with his redeeming only the sinners. Of course, that's a "dynamic" which turns top to bottom: "When I am weak, then I'm strong." And thus one becomes a dialectician of life without having studied Karl Barth! Darling, you ought to know that I am fine, that I am not sitting here as a grumbling Ajax, but as a joyful disciple of Christ, and that I am led on the path where we become "like children." My love to you and everyone. Always,

Your Martin

1. Dr. Walther Seelmann-Eggebert was a member of the Dahlem congregation.
2. The attorney Adolph Bunke was expelled from Silesia and led the Confessing congregation in Glogau.

November 8, 1937
To Mrs. Else Niemöller

My dearest Elslein!
All sorts of kind letters, dated the 5th, arrived today. But you and the entire "family," excepting Pauline, were missing. So I'm hoping for tomorrow. And it's only two more days till I see you myself. I am looking forward to it with my entire heart. As I write to you now, the attorneys are probably at the ministry; but I don't believe any decisions will be reached there. Sometimes I think of our game we played as children: "One, two, three, who's got the ball?" But I am quite cheerful about it. It occurs to me that you ought to go personally to G.[1] and as mother of your seven children demand that the public charge of treason against their father be withdrawn since it's quite easy to establish that not one word of the kind was ever said. The same ought to be demanded of Meyer.[2] I once wrote to you about this before; did you ever discuss it with B.[3] or Colonel Sch.?[4] Yesterday, Sunday, came to a very quiet close; I am deeply engrossed in Macaulay. Couldn't a second-hand copy be found (Tauchnitz)? Ask about it at Warneck's; I think I might like a copy for Christmas. And chapter VII contains things about James II's church measures which are of such current interest that every theologian ought to read them today.

In Elberfeld they are celebrating father's birthday now; last year Wilhelm drove over for the day. I certainly hope we can both be there at his eightieth in two years! God only knows for sure! Are you at Käthe Dilthey's today? Asmussen sent a card; he did not receive my message in the L. matter; I assume, then, that it must have landed on Ch.'s desk![5] Farewell, my darling; I hope the children are all well, and the troubles in the parish are quite overcome?! Let us continue to practice

74

patience: "Grasp thus the faith, the hope and the Holy Cross together; for each follows from the others!" (Luther). Faithfully,

Your Martin

1. G. refers to Hermann (Wilhelm) Göring (b. 1893), minister president of Prussia starting in 1932; and from 1935 high commander of the Luftwaffe and holder of many other offices.

2. Otto Meyer (b. 1888) was director of the German News Agency and resident in the Fehlendorf section of Berlin. He had once been a naval officer.

3. B. refers to ministerial director Dr. Ernst Brandenburg.

4. Colonel Martin Schulze, formerly of the Imperial Navy, rendered Martin Niemöller the most valuable and loyal services in the first phase of the church's battle. He was willing to assume any task and performed his voluntary work with a high degree of modesty.

5. Ch., on whose desk Martin Niemöller's card may well have landed, was the chief of the secret police for Berlin—a man who always introduced himself as a pastor's son, who always made references to Romans 13, and who performed the duties of his office severely and insensitively. His name was Chantré.

PART II
November 10, 1937
through
December 4, 1937

With the letter to his wife of November 14, Niemöller turns his attention more directly to the state of affairs within the church. In this sequence of letters, Niemöller makes frequent references to the "spread of confessionalism," to various church synodical meetings, the growing number of pastors being arrested and imprisoned, the important World Conference on Church, Community, and State at Oxford in 1937, and to a brief break in a relationship that Niemöller has with a Pastor Röhricht. This section concludes with a brief but fervent Advent greeting to his colleagues in the Pastors' Emergency League.

The "confessionalism" matter is fraught with complex theological issues, but in practical terms it involved a deep rift between the so-called German Christians and the leaders and members of the Confessing church over the question of who represented the authentic German Evangelical church. Following the synod at Barmen in May, 1934, at which the Confessing church came into being (see Introduction, p. 8), Germany had in effect two Evangelical churches, the Confessing church and its leadership versus the church authorities and those congregations loyal to Reich Bishop Müller.

The rift was most deeply visible at the level of the local districts and congregations (see Niemöller's letter of November 10 and his remark that "the church is built out of the congregation"). In general terms, those churches that adhered to the precepts of the Confessing church became known among Confessing church leaders as "intact churches"; they included a majority of the district or regional churches in Bavaria, Westphalia, and Württemberg and to a lesser extent the churches in Hannover, the Reformed church in Lippe, and the United church in Baden. The "disturbed" or "destroyed" churches were those that fell under the control of the German Christians (see the letter of December 12, Part IV). The general situation within the church after 1934 was a fluid one, with many pastors, congregations, and individual members torn between the two opposing groups, while many others remained essentially neutral in the entire fray.

Niemöller's references to synodical meetings and to the "Council of Brethren" (the ruling bodies of the Confessing church and the Pastors' Emergency League) have largely to do with the affairs of the Confessing church. The World Conference on Church, Community, and State at Oxford was important because the situation in Germany in general and in the German church in particular was expected to — and did — come under intensive scrutiny at that meeting. Niemöller, superintendent Dibelius, and other Confessing church leaders were to attend as representatives of the German churches, but the government seized their passports on the eve of their departure. Ultimately, only three delegates from Germany attended, one being Bishop Otto Melle of the German Methodist church. Niemöller expresses his ire that a leader of such a small denomination should end up representing the German church (see the letter of November 21). Melle's address to the conference was also a source of much criticism among Confessing church leaders. The conference itself, however, passed a strongly worded "Message to the German Churches" which supported the stance of the Confessing church and denounced "the suppression of national minorities as a sin and a rebellion against God."

By the period of these letters, over eight hundred Confessing church pastors had been arrested and many others had been brought in for interrogation, their houses and offices searched for incriminating materials, and their church meetings interrupted by the gestapo.

November 10, 1937
To Mrs. Else Niemöller

My dearet Else-child,

I just appeared in court as a witness against the postcard swindler of Dahlem; fortunately, it didn't take very long. And I found it very interesting to recognize an old BKer* in the district attorney. Just an hour earlier, Christa Müller was here for an official call which gave me no end of pleasure. So now I'm writing you for Sunday, and outside the sun is shining as if it were a delayed summer day! The heather in our exercise yard is pretending too; it's growing fat green buds! So my soul is in a very mild and friendly mood and wants to reflect the rays of the sun that strike it.

Nevertheless, my load is heavy: this morning your card dated Friday arrived and the letter of Saturday. Now I am worried about Wilhelm and, to top that, the old parish trouble is starting all over again. And I was just getting to the point where I could say to myself: I needn't trouble God about my liberty anymore for the congregation's sake. But perhaps (I hope) my view is too black, and by tomorrow you can push some of those clouds away again. Till then I must have patience, and everything will work out! If I only knew if I had to write Wilhelm in the hospital? But you will be seeing him and will deliver my first greetings personally!

Your news of the children did me good. I received written greetings from all of them today—except Heinz Hermann. Brigitte wrote very cheerfully; I had promised to visit her in Weimar with the car as soon as my stay here was at an end. But she seems to see the day foreshortened in perspective and has already started to remind me of a barely-made promise! Jochen writes just splendidly (and I don't mean his handwriting!) and in such a pastoral manner. He received an excellent

*Bekennende Kirche (Confessing church).

79

inheritance from your father, and it is a dear thought to me that all his good feeling is now directed to you. . . .

Jan writes from the Dohnas,[1] Hertha and Jutta from the Pietschkers; shouldn't this be called "sponging?" I'm looking forward to Tini with as much pleasure as a child before Christmas. Good that you wrote me Landois's opinion! Things do progress slowly!

I want to write Jutta tomorrow for her birthday; I think so often of the hour when the child was born, and we were so alone! We have really gone through an awful lot together in these 18½ years; and sometimes I think of our little dead Christine, especially today when I received a long letter from Professor Delekat in Dresden[2] "about the birth of our eighth child." Very touching, but how in the world do such rumors get around? Apparently, there are a few others in circulation as well, as I found suggested in a card from Edzard Jannasch. Lady Rumor, about whom Virgil has such pointed things to say, is very tenacious of life and not too terribly precise about the number and origins of her children. But one really ought to say a word about and against this sort of thing! It seems to be a burden on the morale of my lawyers also, and they have urged me not to write you certain things. But I told them that you had to know everything; otherwise, the whole business would be no fun for me anymore. Laughing with me, they finally agreed; but you will please help me on this point. One of them told me of a story making the rounds in East Prussia that you all suffer great deprivation! Such nonsense must be stopped, especially since it clouds the real point at stake in all this! I am still receiving many greetings from all over the country, partly delightful but partly also anxious ones that cause concern. A pastor's wife from the Mark [Brandenburg] writes of the fatigue threatening many pastors; Diem[3] writes of the confessionalism spreading in the west! These are the true dangers to be remembered and thought of at the present.

I did not fight for the Lutheran theologumena but for the church of our Lord Jesus Christ, for the attacks today are not against Luther; and if Calvinism is decried nowadays, then it is not Calvin who is meant but the Lord Jesus Christ. Anyone who denies this and compromises on this point wields a treacherous dagger and betrays the Son of Man with a kiss!

Tell Asmussen of these worries of mine! Personally, I am well, although daily I receive greetings wishing me a "quick reinstatement!" I suppose this is also the sort of thing that shows people think of me with love, but it also has its negative side: poor old Niemöller! And with this thought they then plead for a retreat to a "Siegfried position." It's well-intended, but I wish God would beat these sympathetic souls with a deaf, dumb, and blind devil, so they can cause no mischief. I am surely well when the brethren stand firm (1 Thessalonians 3:8),** and I am unhappy when I am struck by the longing and the urge for the fight. For then, my spacious cell becomes too narrow! Personally, I intend, first of all, to take up the fight for my honor: I have had myself crossed off the crew list and am considering directing a similar request to the Naval Officers' Association.[4] Then, later, I can apply for reinstatement and then we'll all see where the courage of men lies! Everything else must develop, and in the process I feel like a rather unconcerned but very interested spectator. I do not believe that a solution to the church question can even be imagined within the framework set by attempts made thus far: how fortunate that at this time Wolff[5] from Aachen rather than Zoellner[6] has prevailed in the church's constitutional synod assembly.

"The church is built out of the congregation." If we stay with Augustana VII,*** this is the only possible, practical consequence. And Augustana VII rests on the word of God. Bishops, too, have their mandate solely from the congregation, as Luther understood it. In this matter, there's no use in essays such as the recent one in *Deutsche Justiz*. This kind of lengthy incarceration does make things clear and unequivocal to the conscience, where before one has carried around a lot of ballast! But, I see I must move on.

I was pleased to hear from Christa Müller that they all look up to you because you are so brave; it was a soothing thought. For you know my (theoretical) preference for ecclesiastical celibacy, but there's just no formula for such things.

**"It is the breath of life to us that you stand firm in the Lord."
***A reference to Article VII of the Augsburg Confession which deals with the nature of the church.

And I hope you are not the exception which confirms the otherwise valid rule. Greet the entire house for me, especially Wehrhahn, too, who wrote me another very, very decent letter. All my free thoughts circle around Wilhelm now; God help him and us! "Things go as they go, your Father up on high knows good counsel in all things!"

A heartfelt kiss, my dear!

Your Martin

1. Countess Dohna lived in Berlin-West. Her son was a friend of Jan Niemöller.

2. Dr. Friedrich Delekat was, at the time, professor of religion at the Technical University of Dresden and became a member of the Council of Brethren of the Evangelical Lutheran church of the Free State of Saxony. Later, he was forced into retirement (1936); after the war, he became a university professor in Mainz.

3. Pastor Hermann Diem (b. 1900) was a pastor in Ebersbach, one of the leading men of the Ecclesiastical-Theological Society in Württemberg. In 1955, he became a professor in Tübingen.

4. The deletion from the crew list of sea officers of 1910 was probably due to Martin Niemöller's futile expectation of support from his fellow officers. The same was true of the Naval Officers' Association.

5. Dr. Walther Wolff (b. 1870) was a pastor in Aachen and, beginning in 1919, the president of the Evangelical church in the Rhineland. The constitutional assembly of the Evangelical church of the Old Prussian Union concluded its work on September 29, 1922. Article Four of the constitution includes the important statement: "The church is built out of the congregation."

6. General Superintendent (Dr.) Wilhelm Zoellner (1860–1937) who was greatly respected in Westphalia, had been at the head of the Reich church committee from 1935 to 1937 and had failed in his attempts to unite the Lutherans with the Old Prussian Union.

November 14, 1937
To Mrs. Else Niemöller

My dearest Else!

It is Sunday again and I imagine you are on the way to Jannasch's service. For my part, I've already read the pericopes this morning which are topical enough and then engrossed myself with pleasure and profit in Sass's speech: "He who wishes to arrive at the goal must not shy from the path" (hymn 236). In recent days Macaulay has been a great source of joy and aid to me; you really ought to read chapters VII and VIII, and not only you! Until now I had really had no idea of the decisive relationships of the year 1688; there is really a lot to be learned from the effects of reciprocal relationships: government, church, law, people! I've been at it every spare minute.

Now the bells are ringing outside, and I remember as if it were aeons ago how I shirked or would have liked to have shirked preaching. That is sure to be different in the future! Although sometimes I feel I'd prefer a journey to the sea like Jonah. . . .

By the way, I had a visit yesterday from my lawyer Koch, this time quite affable and cheerful, after we had aired our views thoroughly on Thursday. You're bound to notice the change in Holstein too, when you see him. The gentlemen were constantly concerned with means to end my imprisonment, and—after I had thrown off my "psychosis" which was, at least in part, caused by it all—I explained to them that most important for the church and for myself was the day in court. The title "lawyer for the defense" appears to its holder to suggest a defensive attitude but any soldier knows that any defense that hasn't the force to develop into an attack can lead at best to a cease-fire, never to a decision. Once again, it's no coincidence that I was and have remained a soldier! So, yesterday passed by quickly. In the afternoon I received the books with a handwritten note from Eisenhardt: everything was in order and you must give E. warmest thanks for all his efforts. Now I'll take a break til this afternoon.

And continue now at 2:30 P.M. after lunch and my midday rest. How might Wilhelm be? . . . Tell me: Is H. Hermann coming home for Christmas? And what kind of a gift would you like? I'm not quite in a position to seat myself under the tree for you this time; but I can certainly reach Santa Claus by mail to get him moving. You know my wish already, and I've got something else to add: In a quiet corner of the wine cellar not disturbed by everyday use, hide three bottles for the day of my return: a Steinhäger, a good burgundy, and a semidry champagne. I fear otherwise to be caught quite unexpectedly high and dry. You see, I still have a head for business. The coffee here happens to be really very decent, and I drink a cup every morning and afternoon, not without a kind of hedonistic enjoyment. But I do think back sometimes to the day in London (1909) when I concluded my abstinence of a year—it was an ethically erroneous path—at the Old Gambrinus with a large glass of Munich beer. My present involuntary abstinence shall end with a cheerful imbibing too, when the time comes. Theologically, I've come a step further: I found—here of all places—the following words of Luther: *"Vinum est benedictum et habet testimonium in scriptura, cervisia autem est traditio humana."** Perhaps your Latin is still sufficient for this; if not, ask Sass for a translation! Isn't that really charming? The only question is what good Martin thinks of Steinhäger! I suppose only Asmussen would be able to provide the information. And you could pass it on to me on some future occasion. . . .

And now remember to arrange in good time your visit on the 22nd—tomorrow in a week; the pleasure of expectation can begin anew. I hope that by then the sky will be clear again! On the day of penance we'll be having a service and communion; I suppose Jacobi will do the honors for all of

---

*Luther's words are: "Wine is blessed and has its testimony in the Scripture; beer, however, has only human tradition on its side."

you?! Many thanks, my dear, for representing me so well. Now you'll be preparing for the helper's party (with good Countess Pfeil!); may God grant you the necessary breaks and fresh strength daily, as we read in Isaiah 40:31.** Give everyone my greetings; a warm kiss for you.

From your faithful Martin

** "But those who look to the Lord will win new strength, they will grow wings like eagles; they will run and not be weary, they will march on and never grow faint."

November 17, 1937
To Mrs. Else Niemöller

Dearest wife!
I've just returned from the communion service and want to use the time left till noon to get started on your letter. We sang hymns 140 and 135, heard a sermon on Psalm 51:12; there were about 250 of us men, and lots of youths who were around or under twenty! I also saw the brother of Perels[1] (the pastor from Mark Brandenburg) who must belong to a new series.[2] For us pastors it's surely good and beneficial to be thus placed in the community of the "publicans"—those cast out from the world and pronounced to be *sinners*! I won't easily forget this day!

By the way, I hope this was the last "day of penance" fulfilled in the church services. This "holi"-day was declared in its time by the Prussian *state,* and was always a crux for the *church*; and if I had been at liberty I would have worked this year to drop it. Do have Niesel put it on the agenda for the next Prussian synod.[3] . . .

And Monday we'll be seeing each other again—four more days. It's a bit like 1919 in the first year of our marriage, when we used to meet Sundays in Western-Kappeln and be apart for the rest of the week. Only in those days we had more than fifteen minutes at a time and we didn't have Aunt Lilli sitting guard over us every minute! By the way, what do you think of a vacation with "Katharina"[4] in Münsterland? Or Lüneburg Heath—this is the right time of year. Only what about accommodations? I've had enough of my hard couch, and my soldier's memories are but a fox's consolation in sight of sweet grapes. It's good that I haven't any other problems; in fact, I'm amazingly well compared to two months ago. And I wish I could transfer a part of my well-being to your worried existence! The sheet is full, more tomorrow. You know that I love you, but I do want to assure you of it expressly again! Faithfully,

Your Martin

1. Perels is the Reverend Dr. Otto Perels (b. 1908), a pastor in Rehfelde, a brother of assessor Friedrich Justus Perels who was born in 1910 and was shot on April 23, 1945.

2. A "new series" of arrests occurred at that time only in eastern Prussia, where no fewer than forty-eight pastors were in prison on November 9, 1937. At the same time (beginning November 7) five Brandenburg pastors were in jail with Perels.

3. The "day of penance" was, to be sure, always ordered by the *Summus episcopus* on particular occasions, for example during times of great suffering or on the outbreak of war. The conference of Eisenach attempted as early as 1852 to bring about a common policy for the German churches. But in 1878, 28 different churches had 47 different "days of penance" on 24 different days. It is clear that the topic of the day all too often was determined and evaluated by political concerns.

4. The Niemöller family automobile.

November 19, 1937
To Mrs. Else Niemöller

Dearest Else!
Today, Friday, your card of last Sunday arrived with several other pieces of mail, all quite gratifying; even Hermann came through with a card again. It appears that there's quite a bit more to happen before Christmas; from Bochum I hear that young Bodelschwingh is in prison too. One wonders what the intentions of the ministry for church affairs are; Zoellner's last words come to mind again![1] Good that we know him who holds also these matters in his strong hands and without whose will nothing occurs. Now it's two more days till we see each other again. . . . My lawyers visited me this week, and that was good, although nothing of importance happened or is about to happen; I don't believe that my court date will soon be finally set; but I'd be very happy to be wrong about that. . . . Regards, my love; I'm looking forward to seeing you. Most warmly and faithfully,

Your Martin

1. General Superintendent Dr. Wilhelm Zoellner had been abandoned by everyone, even the bishops, and did not long survive his resignation forced by Kerrl (reichsminister for church affairs). Zoellner died on July 16, 1937, in Düsseldorf. Martin Niemöller visited him before his death. Zoellner said to him, in effect, "Damned is the man who relies on other men." Niemöller had reminded him that he had warned him against trusting the Lutheran bishops.

November 21, 1937
To Mrs. Else Niemöller

My dear, dear Else!
I've just come from church; we had services after all which
I found a pleasant surprise. We sang hymns 311, 175, and
317; P. Lemke[1] held a sermon on James 1:12 and Romans
14:8. It was really quite decent, even if the main thing is always
missing; but it forces itself inevitably into one's consciousness
in the hymns and verses, so that the absence is bearable. And
outside the sun is laughing over this "Sunday of the Dead,"
and people are gathering in hordes at the graves; but they'll
receive no ounce of Christian consolation: "Culture permitted;
propaganda prohibited."
But the living one goes through locked doors, and neither
rock nor guards can keep him in the grave. I'm under the
impression that in ten years we will have a young generation
who will not only not join the battle against the Christian
faith, but will transform it into a battle against the new myths.
No covering up or hushing up will change a thing. I read
Heckel's[2] clumsy piece of work in the *DAZ* today which appears to have taken in the southeast European German
churches, though only an excerpt is printed. And the *DNB*
contains a highly inept declaration by the German Christian
"bishop" Diehl of the Palatinate[3]—how can one complain about
an "insufficient understanding of the German church" at Oxford, if German participation has been forbidden or refused,
and all of German Protestantism is represented there by the
Methodist bishop Melle?[4] In 1909 the German Methodist
church had all of 20,000 members; today they may double
that number, but that is not one tenth of a single Berlin *district*
synod! The "bishop" has approximately the same jurisdiction
as the administrative pastor in Berlin's Wilmersdorf! But nat-

urally the public has no notion of this. "There is nothing hidden that will not be revealed, and nothing secret that will not come out" (Mark 4:22). Enough about that!

Yesterday noon I received such mail, including your cards of the 15th and 16th and the letter of the 17th. Many and happy thanks; I will learn personally how Wilhelm and the children are from you soon. Röhricht is truly a peculiar saint;[5] he should be allowed to pursue his own ways in his district and in business matters. He has no supervisory rights by proxy over Sass and Sass is not to yield an inch! The available pastors have equal rights to the services in the congregation, and he has no business poking into that. You must hold out to him the prospect of creating district women's auxiliaries for Center and North. I hope he'll be reasonable again then; better yet, start afresh with it! Just don't stay on the defensive! Basically, of course, I'm sorry for the man; disappointed ambition is always a bad counselor. . . . But apparently it's to no avail to try to reason with him!

I've all sorts of concern about the children who are to be confirmed; should my imprisonment stretch out for months longer, which we must consider, then have Wilhelm confirm those who can wait no longer. I promise the others that I will take them in thoroughly (two to three times a week) for four weeks after my release, and then confirm them without considering the church calendar. You can tell them this now so that the parents have time to think about it in peace as well; for time does fly and it's better to take steps in time rather than fail later when everything is helter-skelter. Now then for my lunch break!

In the meantime I've eaten and slept well (it's 2 P.M.). What might Susanne Niesel be doing?[6] I hear that her Wilhelm is in prison again too; and I hear the same about Putz.[7] On the other hand, Steinbauer is free again.[8] Fritz Müller, too, indicated that he was prepared for arrest. Strange times and strange people! And in the meantime we are rapidly approaching Christmas, which has always been a festival of peace: Christian holiday or pagan solstice? I am curious to see how our friend Silex will wiggle through!

Couldn't you do your Christmas shopping with Susanne? Then you could help each other over the low spots. You'll have to buy the cups, finger bowls, and bread box by yourself; I'm somewhat unhappy at not being able to prepare a surprise for you; perhaps Brigitte can come along to the visiting hour on December 21 so that I can have her to myself for the last five minutes. Asmussen wrote me very kindly that he might drive you out during Christmas week; I keep asking myself whether it wouldn't be better to take up our original plan which we were quite agreed upon till July 1st? In the present course of things the children are deprived of an orderly development, and you will be at the end of your strength one of these days. This kind of an interim solution is really only viable for a limited period of time. You have always written me a categorical "no," but you haven't given me your reasons. I'd be very happy to be in the wrong; but I was right about this business with Röhricht although you kept reassuring me! If ministerial director Brandenburg should want to see me about *that,* then I will welcome his visit; but please call off any other visitors, or else, see that it is known that, besides family members, I want no other visitors *without prior written agreement.* In any case, you, dear, should take a two-hour afternoon nap, since you can neither get to bed before midnight nor get up after eight in the morning. If you are "fidgety" although you've hardly a child at home, there will be a catastrophe which no sympathy from the congregation and no society of friends will alleviate!

About myself, I've only positive things to report; the beer source is still dry, but that will come. My appetite and my sleep are still fine. I'm now deep into Volume IV of Macaulay! Also, I've begun to read Luther again. The only problem is the mail; it's simply becoming impossible to answer it all. I think I need to have cards printed up, although I've sent off no two identical cards of thanks yet. I'll wait another week, though. But no situation is perfect: "Where you are not, there is happiness!" Heinz Hermann wrote two cards this past week! The second was somewhat better than the first; which I believe I mentioned. Any other family matters we'll talk about tomorrow, I look forward to it *greatly*! I had good news from my parents and from Pauline too. Gudula copies out the entire "Song of the Sun" of Saint Francis in a notebook for me: an excellent job for the little thing! She appears to have inherited "the final touch" from her mother. Wehrhahn sent another very decent letter. Please say hello to all the young folk from me, including Kuhlchen, Elsie, Dora, and Grete.[9] My thoughts are always with you: even he who is buried alive awaits resurrection, and every day brings it a step closer! Deeply and faithfully

Your Martin

1. Prison Pastor Paul Lemke (b. 1883).
2. Bishop Dr. Theodor Heckel (b. 1894), named to be head of the church office for foreign affairs and granted the title of bishop by the German Evangelical church on February 23, 1934.
3. The bishop of the United Protestant Evangelical Christian church of the Palatinate was Bishop Ludwig Diehl (b. 1894).
4. Bishop Dr. Otto Melle. On his role at the World Conference of Churches in Oxford, see A. Boyens, *Kirchenkampf und Ökumene 1933–1939,* pp. 167ff. and 359–63. His speech at that conference is quoted in *Junge Kirche* (1937), pp. 642f.
5. Pastor Eberhard Röhricht (b. 1888) had been a colleague of Niemöller and Friedrich Müller at Dahlem since 1927. In 1935 he turned his attention to the political affairs of the church bureaucracy. After 1938 he was a part-time member of the council of Mark Brandenburg.
6. Susanne Niesel is the wife of Wilhelm Niesel. The arrest mentioned here occurred sometime soon after November 9, 1937. In all, Niesel was arrested nine times.
7. Pastor Eduard Putz (b. 1907) was also arrested after November 9.
8. Pastoral vicar Karl Steinbauer (b. 1906) had been arrested earlier. His name was on the intercession list of November 9. At the time, he was vicar in Penzberg.
9. "Kuhlchen" is the head of the congregation office, Miss Else Kuhlmann; Elsie is Miss Else von Stryk, later the wife of Professor Dr. Karl Gerhard Steck.

November 22, 1937
To Mrs. Else Niemöller

My dear heart Else!

I have not yet quite gotten over my fright at your appearance; but your air was really bright and cheerful, and that calmed me down somewhat. But now I do ask myself whether it is right that you remain in Dahlem. If you insist on staying, you *must* take better care of yourself, and I cannot decide if that is possible. In any case you should know that I'd be just as calm knowing you were somewhere else, but were in relative peace! I forgot to ask you about Niesel today; the baby demanded too much of my attention. On December 1 I'd like you to come again alone; but it was lovely anyway!

Today your card of the 18th arrived, and one from Bartning too.[1] Unfortunately, at this point there's no use in my answering any longer; if they want my opinion, they will have to ask for it *first,* then call the meeting. I refuse to cooperate with R.[2] as long as the letter of September 30 has not been retracted. And anyway, according to the principles of the Prussian church he has no business in the Council of Brethren in the first place. I will not even consider yielding so long as he uses my imprisonment to impede the gatherings of the congregation (Dibelius, catechism evenings, preaching substitutes). Let him do his business and leave us to do our work! I did not want the fight, but I will not shy away from it either. I do not wish Diestel's visit without a prior written understanding; please let him know this in all friendliness. Bartning writes that he was here on the 18th but didn't get to see me; circumstances permitting, his visit would be valuable to me! The main thing, I suppose, is that Wilhelm take the pamphlet in his hands again. I'm sorry to have to write about all this; the other things will get their turn again tomorrow! And now,

93

farewell, my dear! Give my heartfelt love to all, especially Jochen, whom I only saw "peripherally" today! Warm regards and a kiss from

Your Martin

1. Professor Ludwig Bartning (b. 1876) was the church master of the Dahlem congregation. He was a pillar of the community, a regular and very independent preacher of the gospel. His essay "Martin Niemöller's Berufung" in *Bekennende Kirche: Martin Niemöller zum 60. Geburtstag* (Munich, 1952) belongs among the most beautiful things ever written about the Dahlem pastor. Bartning died on December 27, 1956.
2. Most likely Röhricht.

November 23, 1937
To Mrs. Else Niemöller

Dearest Wife!
Even though I'm not yet through my mail despite two hours of reading (enough is enough, and seventy-three messages in one day is really enough!) I want to stop and write my note to you! This morning Holstein was here; we plan to request my leave to spend the holidays with the family at the end of this week; we—that is you and I—will then let our further considerations depend on the result. I also spoke to H. about the military court of honor (Erler has nothing to do with it!) and about a disciplinary measure of the church (there we'll need Brother Müller!). I am very well, thinking with all sorts of pleasure of yesterday's reunion! The gloves and shawl came through, many thanks! Only they are much too beautiful for this place! Also, your cards of the 18th, 19th, 21st, and the letter of the 20th arrived. So I'm up to date again!
If you're really going to succeed with the morning prayers, you mustn't skip *any*, even on birthdays! When you're there, no one will notice, but should you be absent, everyone will know, and that's something you must count on. Would you send me the letter from Uncle Karl B.[1] or at least an excerpt? I had a fine letter from Mrs. von Rottenburg today; there really are good people still! Mrs. Rigele too sent a handwritten

note, which I found wonderful.[2] About the car: coco [rope] mats are the right thing (not rubber), because of the dampness. The other winter outfittings will have to wait and we'll use the "dough" for more urgent things.

I hope very much that Niesel and Vogel will return soon; I can't believe they'll turn the intercession list into a criminal affair. Everything becomes dull at some point. And the new religion will hardly win new "believers" in this fashion. *Habeat sibi*! May I refer you again to the *Magnificat*, a source of consolation, joy and strength! I've written to Brigitte that I hope to see her in any case on the 21st. Have you spoken to Friedrich Mitz? Now to conclude: You should work hard at school. For Tini I hope that the wound hurries up and heals. Hello to everyone, the little girls too! A long letter came today from Elberfeld.[3] I've now gotten to No. 2007.[4] Farewell, my dear heart; I think of you faithfully and look forward to December 1.

Warmly,
Your Martin

1. The letter from "Uncle Karl B." is certainly from Karl Barth. But it is not easy to ascertain its content; it could be about the World Conference in Oxford, or possibly it is his letter of October 8, 1937, to the acting heads of the Confessing church urging them to resistance against the Third Reich.
2. Mrs. Olga Rigele, Hermann Göring's sister.
3. The home of Niemöller's parents and his sisters Magdalene and Maria.
4. Niemöller had begun numbering the accumulated cards and letters.

November 25, 1937
To Mrs. Else Niemöller

My Dearest!
Although I received mail today (mainly from the 22nd), there was unfortunately nothing from you, so I'll take up my pilgrim's staff again and look hopefully ahead twenty-four hours! My head is a bit benumbed today and I can't risk smoking. But the attack is happily past, and I hope to have a few weeks peace again; but it was really bad! This morning "Uncle Tonne"[1] was here first, and then Dr. Koch around noon. The documents are back and in the process of being taken apart by the lawyers; no news yet about the trial date. But in any case, it is as if, after being becalmed at sea, the first cat's paw breezed across the water and we heard the mast creaking. Only there's hardly to be any progress now before Christmas; and I do have very many things on my mind for the trial now that I didn't in August.

I'm sure you read the speech in Fulda.[2] I'm sure we may say that the first stage is at an end; the young Confessing church has succeeded in preventing the politicization of the church! I'm *very* happy that we have come so far. Well done. And I've gotten the impression that they are not about to renew the attempt. But of course, it is another matter whether this will should prove to be stronger than the internal logic of the mythos!

Is Niesel back again? His affairs and assessor Vogel's are very suitable for me as materials, but it's really not as if we need seek any more! However I want the business with the military court of honor pursued! I am very curious about news from you, my dear; how are things in the parish, when is Wilhelm coming, how are all of you? I received a book today, *Die kommende Kirche* by Lüthi;[3] have you an idea of who sent it? I know nothing. And now farewell, dear, more tomorrow; just five more days! I'll probably have to go at it more with the lawyers now; that's not a pleasant thought. But we must get through to the other side of all this! Say hello to the children, Sass and Wehrhahn, Kuhlchen and v. Stryk, Grete and Dora. And a warm kiss for you from

Your Martin

1. Unknown.

2. Reichsminister Kerrl gave two speeches (in Fulda apparently on November 24 and in Hagen on the 30th) about state subvention to the churches. Both speeches were very sharp and called forth a large response in the newspapers, including the Nazi media (e.g., in the *Schwarzen Korps* of December 9, 1937). For details cf. *Junge Kirche* (1937), pp. 1,034ff.

3. The very topical book by Walter Lüthi, *Die kommende Kirche: die Botschaft des Propheten Daniel* was published in its 10th edition in 1937 by Friedrich Reinhardt in Basel.

December 1, 1937
To Mrs. Else Niemöller

My Dearest Wife!

That was a beautiful reunion this morning, and I hope that despite the haste and brevity of the visit, you are of the same opinion. I am especially pleased that, apart from your outward appearance, you appear to be fresh, at any rate considerably fresher than the last time, and that you intend to take a vacation from the 11th on for a few days. It will also be useful for our possible reunion for the holidays; for then we will have to compress an awful lot into the thrice twenty-four hours! God grant that it works out—and otherwise we will continue to practice patience—for which purpose it doesn't hurt to have a rested body either! Please remember this business with the mail; it's really becoming impossible: today there were again about one hundred pieces. I have taken out your letter (of the 27th) and your cards (28th); I haven't even been able to look at the rest—despite having given up my afternoon nap. Maybe this evening after I've cleaned my cell.

Your letter of Saturday is capital. I am especially happy

about the things you say about Bavaria and East Prussia, while Niesel's report is less optimistic. Even Holstein, who was just here, was quite destroyed by his experiences in Magdeburg. I can't see any of it as tragic; that which has come alive in the church cannot be killed by means foreign to it; and that it gradually will take on the proper form and character—our Lord Jesus Christ will take care of that with or without us. It is but a small addition to the great gift he has already placed in our hands! Fritz Müller has only to concern himself with the church in Prussia, and not view the national "temporary leadership" as the only basis for his reflections![1] Inevitably, that is a dead end now. In my opinion, they should go ahead and allow both a Lutheran and a Reformed Reich synod, but in both cases make sure of a strong Prussian participation by people good and strong, capable of crystallizing the young generation of Bavaria, Württemberg, Saxony, etc. who seek contact with the other "confession." If this opportunity is allowed to slip by, we will again have to spend years in fruitless frontal attacks with the confessionalists, and possibly to wait until they've died out! If Meinzolt[2] is back on the right track on this point—you know that in 1934 he was the sworn enemy of confessionalist attempts to solve the problem—then his "conversion" can be of use. If he has only returned to a personal inclination for me and my tactical-practical stance, then it does not mean much. "It's a good thing that improves!" But enough of all that; just do speak to Müller and Asmussen about it!

You spoke in your letter of the danger of the children's becoming spoiled; I fear the same danger for the parents! I have received old German copperplate engravings from the Bible school; a book about Second Isaiah from Bunzel; a collection of busts of Christ from a Miss Sprengholz (of whose acquaintance I am not even aware). Mrs. Meinecke has announced a book by Rittelmeyer. Where is it all to end? Perhaps I should change to missionary work to avoid all this? . . .

It was nice of Wurm to write to you, even if it did take him an awfully long time; I would just like to know if the idea was his own.[3] He is a good man; the bad young ones of Berlin used to call him the "Christian prayer-book preacher from Stuttgart." But his sermons are fine—should you want to read

98

any, you will find a small volume in the upper right of the oak bookcase. In Württemberg, my imprisonment has contributed toward bringing the "moderate Confessing church" closer to the society again: a new Council of Brethren. I shall be surprised if it holds. I hear little from that corner of the world these days; apparently the news is going around there that I've been at liberty all this time, which unfortunately is a false doctrine of course. In Bavaria too this opinion is making the rounds. . . .

Be well, my dear, dear heart. Tonight I'll sleep well despite the hard mattress. Assure Wilhelm of my brotherly love, and may God grant that Mieze be not too hard hit by her flu.

With love and affection as ever,
Your Martin

1. Niemöller apparently did not think the "board of Kassel" (founded on July 6, 1937), to which the conference of bishops, the temporary leadership, and the council of the Evangelical-Lutheran church of Germany belonged, a useful or productive body. In fact, it never got beyond resolving a message to the congregations on August 20, entering a protest with Himmler about the prohibition of teaching and examination institutions on October 26, and having a declaration against Rosenberg read from the pulpits on October 31.

2. Dr. Hans Meinzolt (b. 1887) was vice-president of the Bavarian Council of Churches.

3. Bishop D. Theophil Wurm, 1868–1953, was bishop of Württemberg since 1933.

December 3, 1937
To Mrs. Else Niemöller

Dearest Elslein!
As I fear a card will not be sufficient, here is a short letter.
First of all, sincere thanks for your letter of the 30th and for
the greetings of Professor B.[1] So you were happy about the
reunion? That makes me deeply happy too.

Now to your correspondence with R[öhricht]. It's a pity
that you didn't ask my advice first. I don't want to stoke the
fire, the point is really to withdraw his sustenance. That R.
makes reference to his good reputation is his right; that I do
it too I think is my duty. No man can judge this matter in
such a fashion that it would be settled. I must establish that
the letter of September 30, for those of us faced with the
responsibility, is in its substance a stab in the back; furthermore, I must say that a *personal* relationship of trust from me
to R. is not possible, after he put his name to the letter of
September 30 *while I sit here.*

The conclusion that I draw is not an attack against R.,
which I'm not interested in, because I wish to leave the matter
as he represents it to itself, but my conclusion is that I want
the boundary line between his work and mine drawn in total
clarity, so that the friction which must drag on (in) the parish
may cease. So preaching, lessons, youth work, women's and
men's service must be in my or my representative's jurisdiction
without interference. In this connection I mentioned the fact
that there ought be no more attempt at a mutual celebration
of the children's service! We *must* go apart, for we *are* apart.
And God grant that we may come together again some day!
Please let the church master know my views on this. The
substantive response to the letter of September 30, to which
I have much to add, will have to wait until after my release;
it may lie in the congregation. I will not change my personal
relationship to R. as a human being and a Christian; that is,
I will only fight for freedom and for the continued existence
of what I stand for, and never against R.; and of course I will
allow interference in this matter only when approached with
clear reasons from the Bible, not with vague grounds for dis-

trust (I purposely avoid the word "suspicion"). Please send me a copy of the letter and the addendum.

There, that's enough for today, my dear. You don't have it easy, but this too must be accepted and overcome! Give my love to Wilhelm and all the children, all our friends, Dora and Grete! I look forward to a week from tomorrow. Isaiah 9:1.* I am grateful to you from my heart and love you.

Your Martin

*"But there will be no gloom for her that was in anguish" (RSV).

1. "B." is the Dahlem church master Professor Ludwig Bartning.

December 4, 1937
To the Brethren of the Pastors' Emergency League

Dear Brothers!

It is quite impossible for me to respond individually to the many hundreds of cards and letters that I am receiving during this Advent; but I do have one sincere request to all of you: Let us not give way to fatigue! Once again, some say that the suffering of our church is a sign of the wrongness of its path. Faith bids us answer that the apostles have shown otherwise. Of course, we know this, and stand by it; as little as our well-being creates or guarantees our peace with God, so little does our suffering do also. Rather, this peace remains the work and the mercy of the one who has brought everything to completeness and perfection in order that we may be called the children of God. Let us believe these joyful tidings of God, and with *their* strength pursue our path toward the one—unconcerned about the censure of other people, and with the peace of Jesus in our hearts and the praise of God on our lips! So help us, Lord!

Your faithful Martin Niemöller

PART III
December 4/5, 1937
through
December 31, 1937

In the letter to his wife dated November 14 Niemöller makes a brief reference to the approaching Christmas season, and in his letter of the 23rd, we learn that Niemöller and his attorneys plan to request a prison leave in order to permit him to spend the holidays with his family. Apparently, such a request was formally made on November 27, and Niemöller's anxiety about its outcome is reflected throughout this section of his correspondence.

The month during which Niemöller wrote these letters was also a turbulent period in the Confessing church. The conflict between "intact" and "destroyed" churches (see the introduction to Part II) had grown more acute, exacerbated as it was by the government's increasing repression of the Confessing church and its leaders. Our attention, however, is riveted on Niemöller's agonizing trauma regarding his family and the holidays. In the letter of December 4 he "doesn't dare . . . believe" that he will be allowed to see his wife and children at Christmas, but the letter to his sister, four days later, expressed the "quiet hope of a visit home for the holidays so that I can see [children] numbers 3 – 6 again." He talks of Christmas presents in his letter of the 16th, but also confesses his doubt that his furlough will be granted.

The letter of the 22nd in which he breaks the news to his wife that the furlough will not be granted, together with those of Christmas Eve and Christmas Day, is one of the most moving of the entire volume. Together, these letters portray a man whose personal anguish can only be imagined, but whose primary concern is the well-being of his family and his spiritual flock.

December 4/5, 1937
To Mrs. Else Niemöller

My Dear, Dear Else!
It is Saturday "evening," or rather four o'clock in the after-noon, and the noise of the day is silenced. So I want to begin my Sunday letter to you, especially since your letter of the 1st came this morning and made me very happy! A few small complaints first: Jochen's letter is only half finished; he writes: "First my report card," then he writes out his grades, then, finished! No signature; perhaps the second half is to follow? What does the list of Advent and Christmas carols mean? Who is the "Navy child" with the drawing of a candle? Who is Jenny Schnell (whose letter I'm returning)? Are *you* going to answer the messages received at home which you give me the addresses for? I can't get through any more, I have arrived at No. 2353! But I am including a card for R.;[1] if you think it right, send it on (in a letter) and *keep a copy*! . . .
So, that's about it! Bartning's visit was a joy for me, now I know quite a bit. Only the end came somewhat suddenly, so that I wasn't able to explain very clearly my position in the R. matter. Perhaps you could let him know of the card. I am *very* grateful to him. Now I am anxious to know how Wilhelm's health develops; he should be careful and, if possible, limit himself to the *ministerium gubernandi** for now. I'm sure you'll let me know soon what his plans are for Christmas. Good that I know everything is in your good hands!
I was happy about Jan's and Jochen's report cards. Times do change—my father would have made a grouchy face if one of us had had these grades! But I am satisfied if I know that the boys are doing their duty. The rest will come in time. Drawing is a particular gift of God; but in penmanship Jan gets a C. The boy just believes the typewriter to be the more

*"the office of governing"

105

convenient solution of the rule: *"o me dareis anthropos ou pai-deuetai"*!** I was also very pleased by the report of your visit with Tirpitz; for once not just bare bones, only you didn't mention Mrs. T.; and how do you suppose the old Serings² are? I think of them often. On the coming third Sunday of Advent the Benckerts in Breslau are baptizing their baby (Katharine Elizabeth); perhaps you could send my youngest godchild a note and a bracelet—a little silver chain with a cross? It's too bad you don't have Brigitte there yet to mother! Could you send me the address of that tall Doctor Gisevius?³ I have never written to him yet; I also have a bad conscience about Wehrhahn. There's just never enough time! Besides, not only the flesh is lazy, but the spirit as well!

So far, I have been spared all my legal documents; I have no idea why Koch doesn't come anymore; I assume he thinks the matter isn't so urgent. There's also been no word yet on the request for leave which Holstein submitted eight days ago today. I don't dare yet believe that I'll be allowed to see you all again at Christmas. But I am cheerful and think back on the visit of the 1st with the same emotion as you do; it really was particularly nice. It's good that your boots for Tiefenbrunn and Oberstdorf are ready; I hope very much that the week will do you good! Give the Schmitts, Golli,⁴ and Mrs. Pietsch-ker my heartfelt and thankful regards, and I hope you'll have clear, fresh, and healthful weather! You must only try to take care of the Christmas preparations before you leave; I will need some new furnishings for the new year: "Shoes and socks are torn . . ."; we'll speak of that Saturday, a week from today. Be well for today, darling of my heart; tomorrow is another day. I love you very dearly.

Now Sunday is here; or rather a good piece of it is already gone. The exercise hour and the service (P. Lemke) are over. The sermon was about Isaiah 60: "Arise, shine, for your light has come. . . ." We sang hymns 347, 6, and 346. You are all sitting in church now; where, and whose sermon, I wonder? The newspaper didn't give any names. Wilhelm certainly can't preach yet, can he? Outside I hear machine gun fire (Sunday,

---

**Roughly, "Give me the self-taught man."

10:45) at some barracks, but I assume it is not the Wehrmacht; it's not exactly conducive to collecting one's thoughts. Nor does it belong especially to national solidarity. Yet: "What's a body to do?"

During Bartning's report, the St. Anne's church was so present to my mind's eye, and how I'd love to be sitting there again amid my congregation! When Lemke concluded reading Psalm 102:14–16*** (without preaching about it afterwards), it really hit me hard! Niesel seems to be worried about "church organization" and the attitude of Müller and Asmussen; something similar is hinted at in the letter from Tiedje and in a card from Kühn of Leipzig.[5] Once in a while I worry a bit, too, that they might let a part of the "Barmen" matter crumble. The congregation will be grateful if we remain firm, and God will call us to account for it. What you wrote me about East Prussia and Putz strengthened me very much, as did a note I received here from an East Prussian pastor in Wormditt prison.

The question of the further development of the "law" applicable to the church has once again become a guessing game. Does no one see how the question of the *possibility* of the "national community" is in danger of being answered in the negative?

I asked you once to inquire about the second husband of Mathilde Ludendorff; did you ever do that? Now I'd also like to ask you for your address in Oberstdorf, so that I can write to you there; on which days—exactly—will you be there? Now you'll be getting ready for the children's service; what are the plans for the Christmas party: who, when where? Are you celebrating Advent at home again today and singing carols? And how does Tini behave, does he already try to sing along? The image of you holding him in your arms and him holding you about the neck is before me and is a constant joy. His tenderness is surely part of the general Niemöller inheritance in him. I have recommended Luther's *Magnificat* to you several times; did you ever get around to it? It is really worth

***"Her very stones are dear to thy servants, and even her dust moves them with pity. Then shall the nations revere thy name, O Lord, and all the Kings of the earth thy glory, when the Lord builds up Zion again and shows himself in his glory."

the while. I have finished reading Acts once again and will turn to Second Isaiah (40–55) in the coming week; that is, if I have the time. I do hope the lawyers will show up again. In Macaulay I'm now finished with the sixth volume; that's really something!

But looking at this time as a whole, I feel like you do: I'm tired of life without you, and when I'm back with you again, I will make *no more* journeys without you, and I'm looking forward to the moment when you will be sitting next to me in the car. Those always were the real highpoints; shut the door and off we go! But let's not be ungrateful for that which is lacking, rather think of what is given to us and remains to us in all circumstances! Say hello to the children! Also Wilhelm, Leni, Dora and Grete, Sass, Wehrhahn, Eisenhardt, Kuhlchen, and Elsie. A kiss for you, my *dear* wife.

Always,
Your Martin

1. Röhricht.
2. The Serings were longtime members of the parish; Professor Max Sering, 1857–1939, was an outstanding economist.
3. Hans Bernd Gisevius (1905–1974) is well known from the resistance movement. In 1937 he was already close to the Niemöller family and made great efforts for many years to counsel and strengthen Else Niemöller and to remove obstructions of all kinds from her path. He also maintained connections with Hans Asmussen and Dietrich Bonhoeffer. In his many publications on the history of the resistance ("Bis zum bitteren Ende," "Adolf Hitler: Versuch einer Deutung," "Wo ist Nebe?" etc.) he also contributed to the history of Martin Niemöller and the Confessing church.
4. Golli is Helmut Gollwitzer.
5. Dr. Theodor Kühn of Leipzig, 1869–1957.

December 8, 1937
To Mrs. Pauline Niemöller Kredel

Dear Little Paulie!
Thanks for your postcard of the 4th. Sorry I don't know when I last wrote you. It is a bit difficult to do justice to all the demands, and so I am relying on the Eberfeld-Frankfurt connection now. The rumors about my health, my decline, and my release have no substance. I feel well and, God willing, intend to live for some time yet. At the moment I have no intention other than a quiet hope of a visit home for the Christmas holidays so that I can see nos. 3–6 again. Still not settled is whether or when my trial will start; but I hope it will come one blessed day! Wilhelm is getting around again— still a bit unsteady. Jutta is in bed with a bladder infection, Tini is almost better. Else is going to Tiefenbrunn and Oberstdorf for eight days. My regards to Carl and your whole clan; God bless you and us all this Advent and Christmas!

Your truly loving brother,
Martin

My Heart Else!

It got late before I could get to my letter to you. I wanted to finish everything else first and it was quite a bit. Toward the end more mail came. It was quite a bit again and so the hours flew by. Now I have your letter of the 4th and the shipments from the 5th and 6th. Sincere thanks! Apart from that everything was very quiet: no attorney, no visits, no excuse.

Inwardly, though, I am very free and happy, and very rich in so much loving sympathy. Contributing especially to that is Second Isaiah which I am reading profitably and with great joy. Bunzel-Breslau[1] sent me the commentary; one can see some signs indicating that the distance within the Confessing church is diminishing. Yes, I have always said: "God the Lord will thrash us together again." The letter from Meiser and the greeting from Wurm point in the right direction; only that "soft-living flesh" from Hannover is not moving.[2] They will come too! From Berlin I have even received a letter from Böhlig who—if my memory does not fail me—was always a centurion for the "moderate" outsiders.[3] The "royal" Saxons are quietly swinging in too. Even Hahn has written.[4] If the effect continues to be that the congregations force a clear position from their leadership (that is clearly what is behind it), then it will be worth my being here another couple of months.

It is good too that God imprisons someone who can endure it physically and bear it mentally, and someone with whom he still has a few things to work in peace and quiet, so that the time is not wasted on him! And whose wife can endure thanks to a congregation which spoils her—even if somewhat turbulently! Yes, it is almost frightening to think of all the love that one can not only not repay but that one can spiritually hardly grasp and take in! I receive greetings from the boys and girls in confirmation class that are full of an unconscious, soul-supporting energy. I stand before it as if beholding a miracle, considering that I give decidedly impartial and sober lessons. Then there are the theology students who write a sermon to which one can only respond on a postcard. Then Hansjochen with all his fifteen years brings one—thank God, unknowingly—to one's senses. And I could go on, and behind it is the living Lord who asks, "Oh ye of little faith, why do you doubt?"

All in all, as uncertain as the line of the visible, external development is—and here I mean my own trial least of all, but much more the apparent collapse of the church's constitutional basis in the current legal discussion—just as clearly we see a new life, the Christian community becoming alive through the word of God. When the *powerful* are silent out of fear or cleverness, the children proclaim God's praise (Matthew 21:16,* Psalm 8:2)** and his power, because otherwise "the stones" would have to cry out (Luke 19:40): "above you rises the Lord, and his glory shines above you." So it may be that we can celebrate Christmas this year with new confidence that "the great joy" will occur once again *to all* people! So love, now you know the general course that I am following. . . .

Your Martin

*"Jesus answered, 'I do; have you never read that text, "Thou hast made children and babes at the breast sound aloud thy praise"?' "
**"Out of the mouths of babes, of infants at the breast, thou hast rebuked the mighty."

1. Rev. Dr. Ulrich Bunzel (b. 1889) was pastor at the Maria-Magdalena Church in Breslau. He was expelled from April 7, 1935, to April of 1936, was banned from print in 1939, and was the deacon of Mittelschlesien (central Silesia) after the collapse of the Third Reich.
2. One of Luther's opponents permanently labeled him "the soft-living flesh of Wittenberg." Here the reference is to Bishop Marahrens.
3. Böhlig is probably Rev. Johannes Böhlig (b. 1877), the pastor of the St. Thomas Kirchengemeinde, Berlin.
4. Reverend D. Hugo Hahn (1886–1957) was superintendent of the Ephorie Dresden-Land, chairman of the Council of Brethren in Saxony, and later bishop of the Evangelical-Lutheran church of Saxony.

December 9, 1937
To Mrs. Else Niemöller, Tiefenbrunn

My Little Else!
I'm already addressing this card confidently to Tiefenbrunn. It is Thursday evening: no mail came today but Koch
and Hahn were with me briefly. So now I am more or less
back in the picture concerning my "papers," but nothing more.
It's to be expected! I'm only sorry about the precious time
that I will have to spend now on this business again. I will
proportion it efficiently though. There is no point in asking
you questions this time. I really would like to know what the
admirals intend but I'll hear from you day after tomorrow—
the same with the crew-evening and whatever else has happened!
I'm so looking forward to your trip and hope that you will
use the days right! Don't let the uncertainty about Christmas
bother you; it is all the more certain that God is guiding us
with goodness and grace. We should be grateful that you can
have all our seven with you and that there isn't one of them
for whom we might not pray and give thanks every day. When
Grandfather Niemöller looked at his brood he used to say
with Jacob (Genesis 32:10): "I am not worthy of all the true
and steadfast love which thou hast shown to me thy servant.
When I crossed the Jordan, I had nothing but the staff in my
hand; now I have two companies."
Yesterday I wrote to Hermann; you must give him my
warm regards. Is it winter down there? In the end you will all
go skating on the pond. My greetings to the beautiful view of
Unering and all of our shared memories related to Tiefenbrunn. And naturally to the Schmitts, Klaus and Mrs. Wen-
gler. "Oh Else, dear little Else, how I'd like to be with you!
Such deep waters run true between you and me!" One day
they will freeze over so we can get across. God protect you
my love.

Intimately,
Your Martin

December 10, 1937
To Mrs. Else Niemöller

Dearest Wife!

It is, of course, a somewhat strange feeling to be seeing you early tomorrow and be writing you a postcard tonight (it is 6:00 P.M.) that will reach you Tuesday in Tiefenbrunn. But perhaps it can still serve as a concrete sign that I think of you constantly. Today your sweet postcard of Tuesday (December 7) arrived; its news pleased me. You have a richer life without me than if I were at home. Would you tell me even more about the crew-evening? It looks as if the navy has decided to start worrying about me a bit now; but without the strong brother it will probably just remain a case of laudable intentions. "Nevertheless: it's a good thing that improves!"

Then I was especially pleased about the news from East Prussia.[1] A general "awakening" like that is good. I heard similar things from Westphalia (Dortmund).[2] Already this half year hasn't been for nothing! And someday one will see that a millennium of Christian culture among our people cannot be liquidated in a couple of years. Even if many do complain about the church, so long as people complain, they still love each other. In a marriage it only becomes dangerous when they are silent with each other. That is an old truth! By which I would not want to encourage this *modus vivendi* for the two of us!

You asked about my condition? Great! Only the cold is not totally to my liking: I need warmer things. My heart is warm, the cigars too; but the rest is only so-so. Yesterday I slept with the windows closed for the first time in 5½ months. No problems with my head or teeth. Good news from Elberfeld; a warm greeting came from the Velberter congregation (P. Herzog).[3] Now, darling, enjoy three days of rest properly.

"Eat, drink, and be of good spirit." Not because we have many things but because we have a good father who wants happy children: "Everything is within his power!" I'm already looking forward to your return and you'll have much to tell on the 21st. Say hello to all the Schmitts and especially to Heinz Hermann. In my thoughts I take you in my arms, dear, dear wife.

Most intimately and truly,
Your Martin

1. Fifty-nine pastors were still in prison in East Prussia on December 5.
2. On the same day there was an extraordinary synod of the Confessing church in Dortmund. Confessing superintendent Fritz Heuner chaired the synod which made a sharp protest against the September 28 order of the S.S. reichsführer forbidding all the education and examination procedures of the Confessing church.
3. Pastor Richard Herzog (b. 1890) of Velbert in the Rhineland.

December 11, 1937
To an Unknown Person

. . . We are becoming a praying church again. And when one sees that, one no longer asks at the sight of locks and bars: Why? How should we otherwise be able to serve our people to whom we have been sent, unless we first learn to pray again for the coming of the Lord! The clearer this becomes to me, the more the psychological pressure and my moderate state of health during these first few months have given way to a happy and grateful confidence. Advent, yes, he is coming! Christmas, yes, we have the great joy of hearing and saying: "A year of grace is nearing its end, a year of grace is intended once again for us." "We should all be glad of this." . . .

December 12, 1937
To Pastor Wilhelm Niemöller

My Dear Wilhelm!
There was only one thing wrong with our visit yesterday: it was too short! Otherwise I would have used all my talents to convince you to stay in Dahlem. Now that that has failed, I sincerely wish that your trip proceeds without any setbacks for you and that you may all celebrate a happy and healthy Christmas. I am not totally at peace either about that or about Dahlem; but God shall help, as he has so often. Today I read about the new regulation that—as far as I can see—is only a makeshift legalization of the state of things which already exists.[1] We must *all* come together once again so that no one becomes isolated;[2] that is the only danger that I see: Acts 27:30–32.* I am thinking of Meiser and Wurm! Talk with Tücking and Koch! True and grateful greetings, my dear, dear brother.

Your Martin

*"The sailors tried to abandon ship; they had already lowered the ship's boat, pretending they were going to lay out anchors from the bows, when Paul said to the centurion and the soldiers, 'Unless these men stay on board you can none of you come off safely.' So the soldiers cut the ropes of the boat and let her drop away."

1. Apparently the decree of December 10, 1937, carrying out the law for the security of the German Evangelical church. This determined that the leadership of the GEC rested with the director of the church chancellory and meant that Dr. Friedrich Werner would in the future unite all the power in the German Evangelical church.
2. By "come together" Niemöller apparently means the call for a Reichs-Synod. Thus also the appeal which is supposed to be directed to its president, Dr. Karl Koch. No new Confessing synod took place, though, because of the opposition between the intact churches and those that were destroyed.

My dear Else,
The whole day today I have been so remarkably amused.
As I went walking early today and an airplane roared away
high over us, brightly shone on by the sun, I looked at my
watch and had thoughts like old Wrangel's: "9:10, have they
hung her yet?" That is to say, my thoughts were congenial:
Whether you were indeed under the safe protection of A.H.'s[1]
bodyguards on the way from Munich to Tiefenbrunn! And
since then the winter's day has been glistening outside: whether
she indeed . . . whether she indeed! I see you with Heinz
Hermann looking over the fields and forests, stomping through
the snow, hear you praising those sturdy shoes, etc., etc. Probably everything is quite different, but I am glad that you are,
for once, to yourself and with your son. I am glad that you
can think of me in calm peace, that no one is standing over
you with a whip, that no telephones or bells are ringing.

You'll be with the Schmitts in Munich when you receive
this card; I hope they don't have a need to "offer" you something, and that you don't get bogged down discussing questions about my trial. I need neither tranquilizers nor stimulants,
and am well supplied with everything. "The torpedoes are
armed" and "all the tubes are ready." As far as I'm concerned,
the way can begin.

Your postcard of Friday just arrived. I hope you've gotten
over your depressed mood. There'll be no moping around
here! Heinz Hermann wrote too; you must give him my special thanks for that. Today Wehrhahn was with me again. I am
always happy to see him. But the defense attorneys don't see

any further ahead than I do; in fact, how tremendously the sense of perplexity seems to have increased in these hopelessly confused church matters! Someday one will have to do what has been avoided since January of '33 and ask the church itself what it thinks of the whole matter. I look forward to that moment; and all this is certainly aimed, in its innermost core, at that moment. Let us then have patience, a passionate heart, and a cool head. A sincere hello to the Schmitts from me, and tell them that I am grateful to them. To you, love, a heartfelt kiss. The separation is bitter. But "worse things have raged through the world." Much joy!

Always yours,
Martin

1. Adolf Hitler

December 16, 1937
To Mrs. Else Niemöller

My Most Beloved Little Else!
Today all kinds of mail arrived, including your postcard of
Sunday (with Gollwitzer)* and your letter of Monday from
Tiefenbrunn. In addition, two postcards came from home
(Sunday and Monday) where Tini is keeping everything in
good order. So I am well up on things. By now Tiefenbrunn's
fields lie behind you again and tomorrow you will be in Oberstdorf. I only hope that you haven't had any overly strenuous
days in Munich yesterday and today. I suppose I'll only hear
about that Tuesday from you personally. It is good that you
could relax at the Gollwitzers beforehand, but wouldn't you
rather have gone to a hotel for the night? Wasn't it dismal
being so alone in the apartment? Were you able to sleep all
right?
Meinzolt should not hide behind Oeynhausen, since, as
far as I know, he wasn't even there.[1] Had the Bavarians taken
the Dahlem Synod of 1934 seriously and clearly adopted the
position that the Council of Brethren is the only church leadership in Old Prussia that we should acknowledge, they would
have spared themselves being accused of dishonorable tactics
and would have spared us much suffering! Instead they had
to cozy up to the fat Abbot of Loccum[2] who has always tried,
and still does try, to satisfy both parties, and who gladly and
intentionally allowed himself to be pushed to the side because
it became too risky! Now we must let bygones be bygones,
although scars remain. God grant only that we have learned
from this. My only fear is that people will start up with Mr.

*As the later content of this letter makes clear, apparently Mrs. Nie-
möller stayed overnight at the Gollwitzers.

118

Werner again.[3] I will certainly hear more about M's visit in Berlin.

So you were actually with Günther Schmitt on your way to T. while I was thinking about you during my walk early Monday. And you are staying in our old quarters (Hildegard's room) with the bathtub that didn't work in those days? I still think of how I wrote letters in that room and how we were brought breakfast in bed! *Quo usque tandem*!? If you're having the same sort of weather down there as we're having here, you can be glad: snow has been falling softly all day today. I have never been in O. Thinking about your car trip to T. on the icy roads made me somewhat uneasy. It's good that you will do all the rest by train! If you still see Dr. Hahn, you must say hello from me.

Yesterday's meeting with the attorneys wasn't merely strenuous, it was also very nice. Koch is an invigorating element. But none of them has any solutions: "There's just nothing one can do." And so in the end it is probably best that the matter proceeds—as our seaman's slang has it—"two blocks" first. Early today Holstein's assessor was here again. People are taking good care of me. Fritz Müller is happily at home again.[4] In Breslau a few brethren are free again, too, as I see from a card the Benckerts sent. Who could have told us all this ten years ago? We truly live in a troubled time. But for me somewhat less "trouble" wouldn't be bad after the last twenty-seven years of my life.

At the moment I'm not hearing anything about congregational matters. Also, I've waited in vain for the decision from the Council of Brethren about September 30 which you wanted to send me. I hope that you can at least let me know about the Tuesday services! We haven't talked with each other at all about Christmas presents, and now there is not time left to do so. We don't want to take up the fifteen minutes on Tuesday with that. You will have to write me at length about it! It is a mysterious thing with my petition for a Christmas visit; I no longer believe that it will be answered. But I am still glad, at least, that I tried everything. Our next visit would then come on the 31st. Perhaps you can bring Tini to me then and not on Tuesday so it won't be all that much trouble for you.

What else should I tell you about me? It looks as if Macaulay ends with Volume VIII, then I'll continue reading Mahon's *History of England*. The mail is a little better at the moment but I fear the Christmas and New Year's flood. Even now I need half the day to answer the mail.

Heinz Kloppenburg has been retired once again by the Oldenburg "Bishop" Volkers; but I don't think that will have any practical consequences! Maneuvers like that still made a certain impression in 1934; what an abundance of authority was frivolously lost then! Bavaria and Württenberg are a bit more abundantly represented in the mail. But, all in all, one has the feeling that down there a church member's first duty is keeping "quiet," and that they still don't, or won't, hear how the ice is cracking. One shouldn't make a principle out of the "Ride over the Bodensee"; that will usually turn out badly!

Ever Your Martin

1. Martin Niemöller's memory did not fail him: Meinzolt in fact had not participated in Oeynhausen Synod.

2. A reference to Bishop Marahrens.

3. "Mr. Werner" was Dr. Friedrich Werner, German Christian president of the Evangelical church high council in Berlin.

4. Reverend Fritz Müller had been imprisoned several days during December.

December 18, 1937
To Mrs. Else Niemöller

. . . I am sitting here completely alone today again. Vogel said he wanted to come, but has not been here. And so I am also somewhat at a loss to know what to think about the petition: there is *still* no response. *Quae cum ita sint,* it seems right to me that you should submit a provisional petition *immediately* in addition to the Villa Ramm[1] visit: "In case my husband's petition for a Christmas visit is refused . . . special visiting privileges between Christmas and New Year with all seven (children) so long as they are together." Address: "To the Special Court II." It would be best to have Holstein compose it. This was urgently on my mind.

Mail came today: forty pieces, some moving and sweet greetings. But I see from my parents' card that Wilhelm is still in Dahlem and that he is not well enough to travel! Strangely, the news about Dahlem that Tini and Sass sent was completely silent on this point. That doesn't contribute to my peace of mind. Well, they have enough to think of at the moment in Dahlem; however, it's unpleasant that I will be stuck in this uncertainty tomorrow and the day after. But it will have to do now.

I'm somewhat afraid that there won't even be any clarification regarding Christmas by the visiting hour on Tuesday. If you receive this letter before then, try to arrange to get hold of Holstein or Koch first so one or the other can try to get some clarification from the ministry, the district attorney, and the court *before* you see me. Otherwise there is not really much that can be done with the visiting hour!

"Oh Century!" . . . I would like to live another three decades in order to present this section of my life with some distance. There is no lack of characteristic material, and humor comes into its own there too. Your description of Meinzolt is classic (I mean *him,* not all the trimmings). Now I am anxious to hear what you'll say about Meiser. Asmussen gave little Hans and Theophil a good grade in contrast to Breit and Marahrens,[2] but he added very skeptically that he was not sure it would last a week. Fritz Müller wrote amusingly: the man has the strength of a giant. He was released Wednesday and then immediately—so I assume from the postcard—held a meeting with the top people. All kinds of remarkable human qualities come to light in these times! Not just shade—light too! . . .

I see then that Rendtorff is preaching in the Church of Jesus Christ on Christmas Day. You will have to go and say hello from me; I find it touching! "And faithfulness, that is no empty madness." By the way, it might interest Admiral Otto Schulze to know that R. is preaching here. He knows him! I daresay that Kloppenburg had to withdraw his promise both because he is going on in spite of his pseudo "Bishop"[3] and to please his congregation. On the whole I believe that this business with the "German Christians" is rapidly approaching its end, even if I am amazed at how quickly—within the course of a year—my allegory of the steps was translated into practice. I am also convinced that not only the preacher of Magdeburg[4] but also many other German Christians will find their way back to the "Confessing church." Lately, whole assemblies of clergymen have written to me from Bavaria and Württemberg. A year ago that would not have been possible. Only God forbid that Thomas Breit or August Marahrens be arrested. That could give the "interlopers" (a fine expression that I found in Macaulay) the upper hand again. Hannover is still asleep, as always, except for the really little corners (Osnabrück, Göttingen, Brome) where we were involved. The fact that these people persevere steadfastly is a special joy for me. And in Schleswig-Holstein it is beginning again. The "Lutheran Council" did create a great deal of confusion. "Yet it shall not be dark over those who fear"—Isaiah 8:23. And the requisite "fear" has already been supplied. . . .

---

1. The reichsminister of justice, Dr. Franz Gürtner, lived in the "Villa Ramm."

2. "Little Hans" is D. Hans Meiser; Theophil is Bishop D. Wurm; Breit is the Bavarian High Council member D. Thomas Breit (b. 1880); and the last named is Bishop Marahrens, Abbott of Locum (b. 1875).

3. "Bishop" Volkners is mentioned only once in the registry of the ministers of the German Evangelical church. He is listed among many other persons as a member of the constitutional committee that met in July 1934 in Erfurt as the "Landespropst Volkens in Oldenburg."

4. The "preacher of Magdeburg" obviously refers to the cathedral preacher Ernst Martin (b. 1885) who belonged to the Old Prussian church committee from 1935 to 1937.

December 22, 1937
To Mrs. Else Niemöller

Dearest Else!

*Jacta est alea,** and nothing came of it. I have just been informed that my petition for a furlough has been refused. The grounds, which I am most concerned about, haven't been given yet.[1] You can pass along my thanks to J. for the fact that after almost four weeks of waiting I at least received the denial a day and a half before Christmas. Without his intervention it would probably have come only Christmas Eve lying under the tree! Next year we will have to try the petition six weeks before the holiday!

I am not sure yet what one should think or say about the whole situation. At any rate there has been no mention thus far of a trial date. Under these conditions I would like to accelerate the matter with the young ones as much as possible and ask you to make the appropriate submissions or appointment right away. I think Superintendent Diestel would be willing and able to help you make contact in England. Holstein was here just now and he will inform you today too. In case I see him yet I'll say he is to tell you not to come tomorrow with the little children but to wait until after the holidays.

If not, we'll let it go as is. It is nice to think back on today's visiting hour. The vacation apparently did help you a little— and how you will need some of your strength again! As things

"The die is cast" ("Iacta alea est,"* Caesar's words upon crossing the Rubicon).

now stand I would most like to suggest that you go ahead and go to England with all our seven, and that Wilhelm should bring his whole family to Dahlem since he won't actually be able to fill both posts! Tini won't be able to get along again without a basic change of climate anyway? Wilhelm or, while he is ill, Susanne Diestel could take care of me with visiting hours, etc. In any case we will have to make some long-term arrangements, so we don't dissipate all our strength. In this regard, we are further along than we were yesterday.

You can tell the parish church council and the Congregation at services my point of view, so there won't be any disturbance when the time comes. Jochen should definitely be confirmed beforehand. You will have to take time to discuss with him at length whether he likes the suggestion I made today or whether he prefers to be confirmed by Uncle Wilhelm or Grandfather N., which would also be very nice for him. Just don't respond to me and to these thoughts—which are not just today's—with procrastinating in mind. Everything here is obviously awaiting a miracle; it is squarely determined that there is nothing to be done until then. You may also, of course, wait for a miracle as we all wait for the Lord's return. Yet despite this and even because of it we must go on managing things as if the miracle will not occur until after our deaths.

So my love, this is a Christmas letter now. We should not focus here on human weaknesses and evils. And we do not want to forget that even the German Fatherland means a foreign exile for us, as for the man who had nothing as he lay in the manger because he laid down his head out of his love for his people!

In the meantime Holstein was here again. So your visit with the children can't be until next week anyway. I impressed the question of the children on him. He was told that the reasons for the refusal were given as: "recurrence risk" (in the family probably?!) and danger of "inciting the community" (as if they could become more restless!). These reasons will doubtless continue to exist as long as I live. And when I asked Holstein if he could see anything at all yet that could bring this matter to a close, he shook his head. So I must assume that they either hope—according to that Solomon-like decision: "Detention is also a form of humbling"—to get me to a "loyalty oath" (that's what one now calls the declarations) or to hold me until some other "miracle" occurs. But perhaps you can be shown another, third alternative by Gürtner personally. *That* visit is timely now, in my opinion. I intend, by the way, to hold out as long as body and soul stay together. And the only thing that disturbs me is the thought that our baptized children could be drawn into the anti-Christian drive partly through our fault, because we are not able to care for them as we really should.

Our next regular visit is on the 31st. As far as I can see though there will not be any visiting hours that day, so you will have to apply for the 30th and then again for January 9. But that is a Sunday, so we should discuss in person whether to meet on the 8th or on the 10th.

Now all of you should take the Christmas sermon very deeply to heart. Over the manger too there is a "nonetheless" of faith written; and the children should sing heartily about the miraculous act of the compassionate God who has been and shall remain our only hope. The congregation's love will support you as it clearly supports me. My special thoughts are of dear Wilhelm, may God preserve him for us and his loved ones, and of little Tini whom I think of sadly with his ailing eye. Will Wehrhahn stay with you now? That would certainly be good! A sincere word of thanks to Aunt Leni for nursing Wilhelm so loyally and devotedly, and to Dora and Grete too who are so supportive of you in all the bustle. It was good that I saw Brigitte today. Tell her—and Jochen, Hermann, Jan, Hertha, and Jutta too—that I love them all from my heart and that I pray daily—more than just once—for them.

Whether or when God will lead us all together again, we will leave in his hand. He alone knows the right time: "He injures and binds up wounds; he destroys and his hand heals!" God send you great strength my love; my thoughts and prayers are like a wall around you.

Intimately,
Your Martin

I urgently need trousers, and money too.

1. There was certainly a good reason for the refusal of his Christmas vacation. The court no doubt anticipated that the gestapo would "kidnap" Niemöller and thereby prevent the public legal proceedings. Later there were many hints that such was in fact the court's fear. Officially, Niemöller's attorneys received the following decision of the special court:

Decision
In the criminal case against Reverend Martin Niemöller regarding an offense against the law of 12/20/34, the petition of the accused of November 27, 1937, for the granting of a Christmas vacation for a period beginning December 24, 1937, is denied.

Grounds for the issuing of an arrest order still exist at the present time within the framework of the decision of the court of October 11, 1937. It is also not feasible in the interest of maintaining public peace and order and, hence, the peace of Christmas in his residential area as well as in the district of his church congregation, to set the accused free for this period.

Berlin, December 21, 1937
The Special Court II
of the District Court
signed Burczek, Dr. Welz, Schwarz

December 24, 1937
To Mrs. Else Niemöller

Else My Heart!
The Christmas bells were ringing outside a half hour ago as I wanted to begin this letter. In the meantime they have become silent and I have had another lovely visit from Rev. Klett, who has difficult duties today. Now it is five o'clock and all of you will be coming home from Christmas vespers, preparing yourselves for the celebration.

I hope that the congregation has calmly accepted the message that I must maintain my stand here "in the interest of the peace of Christmas." And I hope that you have completed the requested action without having seemed in your own eyes to have the role of a supplicant. I am very happy about the "grounds" now. One may say the same thing about them as is written in John 11:51 about the advice of Caiphus: "He did not say such things on his own, but because he was that very year the high priest did he prophecy." And, ultimately, having this matter and its background known will help the Christian congregation of 1938 actually regain its Christmas peace, not endangered today by *us,* and will help the number of those who hear the word of Jesus grow: "Do not fear them. Nothing is hidden that was not revealed." We have not come that far yet, and so I want to do this service, which I must do as God wills it, *gladly* as well! And not merely "bear the unavoidable with dignity."

The bells are beginning to ring outside now again (it is 5:30) and you will be proceeding to opening the "gifts." Will you find enough peace and quiet to give me a detailed report of your celebration? Is Wilhelm far enough along to say a few words to you all? Who will recite the Christmas gospel? "But there happened at the time . . ." Thank God that Rosenberg has not been able to undo this and that these tidings will still live on when no one knows the "general's" name anymore. "The eternal light goes in here to us." "He comes to the troubled, the poor, the oppressed, to those who know 'no other gods,' "—let us believe. He comes for our sake, exactly and precisely for you and me and our children, really and truly for those whose right to exist is denied—without a cock crowing afterwards. He shares their homelessness, their illegality, their "misery." And he does more: he gives faith its legitimacy to stand before the judgment seat of God for his sake. And he gives us knowledge of a home whose doors stand open, waiting for us. And we no longer need to think too bitterly of what others withhold from us, and no longer need to feed ourselves with anger over those who are themselves wretched and, without this child, lost slaves of their fears.

Instead let us announce the joyous message to all: "He saved those who had to be servants all their days through the fear of death!" (Hebrews 2:15). As "shepherds" who have seen the child in the manger and heard the word from the child, we will barter with no "Augustus" and no "Caiphus," but will witness to both whether they would hear and believe "Christ the Lord, born in the city of David." And we praise and glorify God for everything we have seen and heard.

Now it is 6:15; you will be going from table to table, from chair to chair and everyone will be deeply happy for the outward signs of bonds. It will be difficult or even impossible for you in regard to me. I can't even give you a kiss; but perhaps you at least have my letter from Wednesday, written out of a restlessness like that of the shepherd who wants to be on his way. But you will not doubt my being with you because of that. Things are not better for me either. I only have your letter from Oberstdorf, written "rushing off." The one from the 22nd I have seen but haven't been handed yet; and Mr. v. Möller's[1] presence then was so disturbing that I can remember nothing of it. So I have another pleasure ahead of me on the 27th or 28th! Actually though I do have a letter from Elberfeld and Brigitte's postcard from Monday, and an infinite number of other greetings (approx. 320) that I still have to read. And before the week is out, I'll see you again—on the 30th, I think. And I've never looked forward to it as much as I do this time.

I can't have the visit with the children now, under the circumstances, and I hope you will understand—as nice as the whole idea was. I had no end of trouble calming down my defense attorneys again, and good Mr. Koch is really a gentleman who is totally concerned with your position and the treatment given you. Myself, I have already become accustomed to quite a bit, having experienced the treatment given Mrs. Asmussen and the other ladies.[2] How many other brothers might still be sitting at this moment behind barred windows for the sake of the Christmas peace? I, at least, have the great advantage of having my Bible. But the experiences of Jannasch and Niesel[3] have unnerved me deeply; and the judgment of God in Amos 8:11-12 looks upon me with threatening eyes. Woe to our people if no one were there to step into the breach!

Now it is a quarter to seven though; I'll have to think of supper soon, and you will too by and by! Later I will read the Christmas story, begin working on the letters, and sing at the end. Then, when I climb in my bunk you will still be up for a couple of hours, but my thoughts will still be awake too! Tomorrow I'll continue writing.

December 25, 1937 So, dear wife, here I am again. I have

just come from the church; we sang hymns 16 and 19; sermon text John 3:16; reading 1 John 3:1–5. I thought it was strange though that Luke 1 was missing! I suppose you are sitting in church (it is now 10:30) with Müller and the Christmas trees are lit up. Here the whole central hall is *full* of trees in ghastly taste and I am glad that I don't have to have another one in my cell. But I do have a fresh pine branch!

We live in an age that adores the idol of quantity, but even this idol is—as Isaiah says—a nothing.

Just now I was handed the Christmas newspaper. My eyes fell on the caption "Sons of God." I begin to read and am informed that the Galatians are supposed to have been Teutons. Up until now science said they were "Celts." But perhaps both or neither, so what! I am reading the close of the two columns. "That is . . . the historical foundation for an exalted song that begins with Thor's hammer and sings the praise of an eternal life, brought into the world by a child, that extends beyond life in this world, and into which German man has joined in from the first sound on." What did Jesus say to John 5:44: "How can you believe, you that take honor from one another? And the honor that comes from God alone, you do not seek." And Paul writes to the Romans in 1:24–25: "Thus they have forsaken God, . . . they who transform God's truth into lies and have honored and served the creature more than the creator who is praised in eternity."

So we need not be surprised at this "forsaking." When God is robbed of the honor that belongs to him, big words come of their own accord, masking naked fear and cowardice! And everything becomes brittle and frail. I am deeply shaken by what I have experienced in this regard in recent days, and if the Christian community lets itself be drawn into this vortex it will be absolutely all over with our people.

Did you read the newspaper notice about the "Church Ministry's Christmas Celebration"? That is a document: positive Christianity without Christ! The great temptation for us Christians now is the Pharisee: "I thank you, God, that I am not like. . . ." So may the child in the manger preach to us about the simplicity befitting those who receive peace from God purely through mercy. "So you will not become like the children."

129

Because we have not freed ourselves from fear and judgment through our faith, but instead have been *"taken"* with him "out of fear and judgment" (Isaiah 53:8) through the suffering of God's servant so "that *saved* I can glorify joyously" (Psalm 32). And this glorifying of God should preach to those who have heard nothing thus far.

I also wanted to tell you that I read the mail yesterday evening (that is, half of it). It didn't go very well, because the sudden change of weather made me a present in the head— in a new, improved edition for Christmas Eve. But at 9:15 I was given some Veramon and then fell asleep at 10 o'clock without any great pain. Today my head feels a little dull, but is alright again. And my joy didn't suffer; instead I filled in a good portion of the program sung in church. A letter from Diedrichs[4] and another from Röhricht made me especially happy. And my nicest present was an illustrated verse by Käthe Brauer, and next to that was a written and "composed" poem by Mr. Advisor Seelmann—Eggebert! The day before I had a fabulous letter from the submarine commander, Admiral Bauer, but it can't be read without blushing. The ministers of an entire theology school wrote from Bavaria! I concluded with the letter from Mother and Father L. and Lene; Lene writes touchingly, reminiscing about our childhood Christmases. In fact, a number of memories have come up over the last few weeks: partly memories from secondary school like songs that we sang, excursions and strolls with friends. And I am surprised once again at how most of them have died or been killed in war since then! So that I don't forget, one of the special gifts on my table was a dear and happy letter from Wehrhahn. You must tell him that!

Now I'll end my sentence and write the rest tomorrow. It is very nice not to have to write many cards for once. Today I want to treat myself to an afternoon nap, something that just hasn't been possible for a number of days. May you all fare well: "Refuge is with the high God and under his eternal arms."

December 26, 1937 Are you all sitting under Rendtorff's pulpit now? Early this morning I read Luther's devotions and the four pericopes, and sang hymn 350. Then I wrote Mother and Father N. and Pauline. Later on I want to write to the two imprisoned brothers in office, but first I want to finish this letter. Thanks to the cold weather, my head feels significantly better and, besides that, tomorrow the traditional three days will be over.

First, a few messages: 1) I am enclosing a card for you from Mrs. Apholz, a card for Jutta, a poem sent to me from Leipzig. 2) I want to ask you to procure a book for me: *The Message of the Old Testament* (vol. II, *The Book of Faith*) by Hellmuth Frey, in cloth for 4.20 [Marks]. 3) Get three undershorts and three undershirts together for me; I will submit the request for an exchange because everything is falling apart. 4) You will have to take along a number of books and brochures at the next visiting hour, or the one after that. The same with my gray suit. I am still running around in the torn trousers, but I hope that the exchange I petitioned for will be granted soon. I would like to have the gray suit back again soon after it's been repaired, as mentioned, because blue is so impractical. 5) You should have the drawing by K. Brauer-Kreuznach soon after New Year; it ought to be framed.

That's all the requests. Is Ingeborg going to come today and is Wilhelm well enough to be happy about this reunion? And have the children all gotten through the celebration well or did Jan "overcelebrate" again? Just tell me all the details; I am very receptive to that. Today you are, of course, having many visitors again from Dahlem and other communities.

I sent the only copy of the furlough petition to Dr. Gürtner (12/15). Despite the fact that I enclosed a stamped return envelope, the copy still has not come back to me. If you received it, that's fine. Otherwise, though, you will have to send someone from the office to pick it up. I am sitting in the midst of a thousand thoughts and considerations, and ardently wishing for the beginning of January! Do give me, in any case, some clarification about the matter with Mrs. Ludendorff; it would be very valuable to me if I could use that material too right away!

And so I should close for now, my love. This will no doubt be the last you will hear from me until the 30th or 31st. Please, sleep in so you will be refreshed for our fifteen minutes. Mostly, you will tell me about these days and their events, and will have to decide yourself whether you want to bring

Brigitte along or leave her behind. I will mostly just listen. It would be best if you could write down a few sentences about what you have to tell me about the question of the children. I will gladly listen, but don't want to wait and procrastinate. The event of this half year is too clearly before my eyes for that. Then, I also would like some clear information about Wilhelm's condition and the prognosis for Tini. I would also appreciate it if Fritz, as our doctor, would give you his impartial and sober opinion about your condition. Naturally, I always have the feeling that you would like to protect me as much as possible; but that would be a miscalculation.

In the meantime it is midday: do you have guests for dinner today? If so, I hope you will wrap yourselves around a good wine. I'm considering taking an extended lengthy nap because it is cold. Otherwise I am in good spirits and have a lot of "steam in the locomotive." Greetings to the whole house, especially Wilhelm—then all of our organ pipes from Brigitte to Tini, and Leni, Sass, Dora, and Grete! A special greeting to you darling. God send you much strength; he will do it!

Sincerely,
Your Martin

December 26 (3:30 P.M.) This afternoon your greetings from the 22nd arrived. They alone compensate for my staying here over the holidays. A thousand thanks.

1. Schwarz, the district court counsel, had the job of controlling Niemöller's mail. He apparently did this as gently as possible. Not one single letter bears a censor's note; only in one letter were a few words crossed out. After 1945 Niemöller wrote: "Schwarz surely wanted to, and basically did, stand by me and the Confessing church." Mr. v. Möller seems to refer to a substitute; the fact that he had a "disturbing" effect could hardly be changed even though no difficulties arose during his presence there.

2. The wife of Hans Asmussen (Elsbeth) had lodged a complaint, with a large number of other ministers' wives, at the highest offices in Berlin several months earlier in order to get something on behalf of the imprisoned ministers. Their treatment was, in part, miserable.

3. The imprisoned pastors Wilhelm Jannasch and Wilhelm Niesel were denied use of the Bible in prison.

4. Diedrichs was a comrade from Niemöller's crew, and a duty officer with him on the S.M.S. *Thüringen*.

December 26, 1937
To Mrs. Pauline Niemöller Kredel

Dear Pauline!
Heartfelt wishes for your birthday and at the same time sincere thanks for your sweet Christmas greeting of the 18th. Nothing came of the "silent hope"; but perhaps it is better, everything considered. It is easy to be attached—especially around Christmas time—to one's own self and family. But I am sitting here not as a person but as a representative. And the whole affair is exemplary and of basic significance so that nothing would be more damaging than having it get bogged down. But it won't be! I celebrated Christmas happily and gratefully even though I still don't have word from Dahlem. I heard the gospel, hear it daily, and the love of the congregations does not desert me. And it's not this little bit of earthly life that is important in the long run. Love, little Paulie. Sometimes I think of your baptism day, and love has not lessened since then. Greetings to Carl and the children; a heartfelt kiss from your

Martin

December 27, 1937
To Pastor Wilhelm Niemöller

My Dear Wilhelm,
I have just written to Else, and you will both receive these cards at the same time. Please talk her into taking my concerns and worries seriously. I am neither angry nor excited; it is only that I see that this half year of torture is more than enough for the children and their mother and things cannot continue this way without serious damage. Else has already suffered considerably and I notice it in the children, too. They should accept the fact that they will have to be without me for a long time and must be building anew. If the wind should unexpectedly change direction, it will be a small matter; but we have no grounds for counting on that and it would be foolish and irresponsible to do so. I think of you often, dear boy. May God grant you your health again!

In love and loyalty,
Your Martin

133

December 28, 1937
To Mrs. Else Niemöller

Dearest Else!
The day's work is done and all that remains is to send my greetings to you. Gradually I am getting back into the everyday stream, but I am still like one who has been seriously wounded. And I long for a lengthy talk with you because I have the feeling that, for the first time, we do not completely understand one another. The accusation made back then about "treason" was certainly bad; but I was able to defend myself inwardly against that quite easily and rid myself of it quickly, and for good reasons. This matter about the "Christmas peace" is exponentially more difficult for me, not only because of the authority behind these lines but also, and especially, because it entails a judgment about my office and my unsuitability for the office—for which no reasons are given, but it is there nonetheless. I cannot say a word about this myself; others will have to do that. But I also cannot behave to those who wrote those words as if nothing had happened, because I cannot dishonor myself. You can believe that I have prayed over this matter thoroughly and I am still doing so; but I get no further than Mark 15:5, "But Jesus did not answer them anymore."

You know yourself how much I would have liked to have seen the children again, but that is probably one of the beams of the cross that I am now supposed to bear. And the loneliness which I face with this decision is part of it too. I would appreciate a word of understanding from you if it can be honest; otherwise let us bury the subject silently and leave to God what he will make of it. You need not be concerned that this blow will crush me; I take it to him, again and again to him who carried all of our crosses in his. And he does not allow us to be crushed. I am looking forward to your coming,

134

whether it be the day after tomorrow (as I hope) or only on January 3 (as W. thought). The mail did not come yesterday or today. *Juncti valemus*!* God protect you all and guide us mercifully—in the New Year as well!

Devotedly,
Your Martin

*"Together we are well."

December 31, 1937
To Mrs. Else Niemöller

My Dear Else!
Some confusion has slipped into our correspondence. But today, on the last day of the old year, I have to talk with you. I am thankful and glad that I have some peace to do this, although even this thanks and this gladness are not by any means wholly free of sadness.

Of all masks, the "heroic" is the least appealing to me. Also, I think it is the most destructive with its demand of being taken as authentic! Well, it is *real* privation and *real* pain for me to be able to hold your hand in spirit only as we look back on this year that has been thus far unique in our life. Yet the joy of having borne and still bearing this shared burden, of the love and understanding that I have grown along with the difficulties, of possibly growing closer as marriage partners and as Christians because of this separation—this joy is *real* as well. And, in retrospect, we do indeed have cause to join in—despite all the protestations beginning with "in fact" or "actually"—with the chorus "Now thank we all our God" from our hearts.

Today exactly six months are up. And when I think of how only six months ago I could dwell stubbornly on the thought of release for a whole day, I am surprised at myself for actually having to be informed today by the defense attorney that it is a sort of "red letter day" in my imprisonment. I no longer have a need to conjure up a "fata morgana" for myself: six months, nine months, twelve months in order to stay on my feet for the march forward. I know it is possible without such crutches, with the truth of Isaiah 40:31,* and "awaiting the Lord" has nothing to do with stubbornness. . . .

I received your Christmas Day letter and the family's Christmas Day card today, as well as your card of the 28th. The joy was great; please, please do not worry about "becoming bitter"! I wouldn't think of it and would have no reason to do that. There is movement everywhere: a year ago I simply would not have believed that a minister from Hannover, the most orthodox city, would complain about the somnolence of his pious congregation; and I would have had to rub my eyes in astonishment at a greeting from the evangelical youth group in Munich. Somehow in these six months the church's ship has become buoyant again. The paint is chipped, the masts are broken, its whole appearance is not beautiful; but Christ will stand at the helm and the ship floats! Who would have dared hope it when Ludwig Müller thought he had pirated it! It lasted no longer than the red phantom of 1918—and after a phantom like that, one no longer runs away from every ghost but first feels for what is hiding under the sheets! And I think my imprisonment belongs to God's holy humor as well. First the mocking laughter: "We have him now!" And then eight hundred arrests—and the result? Full churches, praying congregations: "World, rave and jump; I stand here and sing in safe peace. God's guard watches over me, ground and chasms must be afraid no matter how much they threaten." To be bitter with all of this would be vile ingratitude. . . .

*"But those who look to the Lord will win new strength, they will grow wings like eagles; they will run and not be weary, they will march on and never grow faint."

PART IV
January 5, 1938
through
February 6, 1938

This fourth series of letters opens on a humorous note, with Niemöller's reflection on a comment by Superintendent (later Bishop) Otto Dibelius to Mrs. Niemöller that one day "people will read about [Niemöller] in all the textbooks on church history" little did Martin Niemöller realize, in 1938, how prophetic Dibelius's comment would prove to be.

The tragic note in this period of correspondence is found in Niemöller's growing anticipation — now that a trial date is set — that he will be released. He thinks it might take months, rather than weeks (letter of January 10), but wants the Pastors' Emergency League to wait until after the trial for an undescribed "big meeting" (letter of January 17) and is already planning to resume his pastoral duties (letter of January 20) and to sort and reply to the several thousand pieces of mail he has been unable to answer (letter of January 23).

In the final letter of this section (February 6) we learn of Niemöller's despair over the prosecutors' decision to exclude the public from the trial and his quandary over whether, under such circumstances, he should refrain from speaking at all during the proceedings. From earlier letters, we know of Niemöller's conviction that the trial would provide him an opportunity to make a ringing defense of the Confessing church and its stance. As it turned out, on the second day of the trial and in response to repeated badgering by the prosecutors, Niemöller refused to testify further and dismissed his lawyers (see the letter of February 8 in Part V).

January 5, 1938
To Mrs. Else Niemöller

. . . Dibelius's writing you that people will read about me in all the textbooks of church history is of little comfort. First, they are boring anyway and secondly, as the Berliners say quite correctly: "What will that get me?" . . .

January 7, 1938
To Mrs. Else Niemöller

My Beloved Wife!
The afternoon coffee just came, and so I will gladly interrupt my work to address a few words to you. The expected ebb in the mail came today. There was only a letter from a young English theologian, a greeting from the Hentschel family from the Burckhardt House, . . . Brigitte's letter of the 4th, and your greeting from the same day. Sincere thanks! Now I am anxious to see whether you'll come tomorrow or only the day after.

My day was very quiet; but I actually sat in a hot bath! The last one like this was in Dahlem on July 1, 1937, an hour before my arrest. I enjoyed it to the nth degree and, above all, am now warm again through and through! Twice I have forgotten to have you send the Conrad family my sincere best wishes.[1] I was *so* happy but I don't want to write myself! Afterwards I'll need some *nervus rerum** again. How are things with the financial situation? Can you handle it? And how will you feel these days after the Pietschker's boys return?[2] Don't

*The meaning is unclear; it is either a reference to Niemöller's need for some "prison items" or for renewed strength.

139

EXILE IN THE FATHERLAND

worry too much about Brigitte. . . . A special hello to Jutta; her cards made me very happy. The boys should apply themselves and accomplish something when they can. At the moment I am being very lazy and am wandering around with you through the country somewhere in the south. But one shouldn't make out the tab without the "proprietor." So I am whistling the tune: "But because it cannot be, I remain here"! Hello to the whole house. But a special greeting to you, love. And I am looking forward to our next reunion!

Always in faith and love,
Your Martin

1. The Conrad family is the family of the ministerial counsel Walter Conrad of the Reich ministry of internal affairs whose book *Der Kampf um die Kanzeln* (*The Struggle for the Pulpits*) was published in 1957.
2. The Pietschker family from Dahlem has already been mentioned several times. Mrs. Ursula Pietschker was a friend of Else Niemöller's. Else liked to invite Mrs. Pietschker and her younger children as guests, and later Mrs. Pietschker often drove Else to her visits at the concentration camp in Sachsenhausen. She died in 1940.

January 10, 1938
To Mrs. Else Niemöller

Dearest Else,

Only a few hours have passed since our visiting hour. Immediately afterwards I was taken to a supplementary hearing, which proceeded, however, without excitement.[1] It seemed to be—for the moment—the last one. This is the coffee hour and I suppose Dibelius is now giving the first confirmation lesson. For me that is both depressing and liberating. Our reunion was so nice! . . .

Don't pay too much attention to the few sparrows who think they are announcing summer. It might be, but it might not be! And the devil works through the burden of disappointment; one cannot allow him to take hold. And don't plan on the vacation too strongly. If I do get out of here, I will have to be treated by Wahn for a few weeks first. And I will also have to preach first, not to mention the confirmations. Incidentally I am counting on it being months, not weeks! . . .

1. New hearings began on January 10, 1938. They were continued on January 13 and 15, this time by the state attorney, Dr. Lange. They dealt with the Prussian Council of Brethren's resistance decisions, especially with the meeting of June 27, 1937.

You Dear Little Else!

The last greeting of the present day belongs to you;[1] I'm thankful that you came. It was a very great joy. I was deeply happy about the children, especially Hertha and her somewhat shy nature but also about Jutta and Jan. Jochen, Jan, and Jutta—the three Js—bear a certain resemblance in temperament and in the way they express their feelings. The same holds true for Hermann and Hertha—the two Hs. And you seemed relatively refreshed to me, although I did notice your "fidgeting"! I think that Sell's visit regarding Hermann and Jochen is a prerequisite to all our considerations about the children.

Your staying with the four boys in Dahlem seems to me right and necessary since Wilhelm's being in Dahlem is out of the question. I will wait awhile and see before I take it up again; but Schmitt's visit doesn't make much sense before then.

You will all be strolling to the Church of Jesus Christ now. In my thoughts I am with you. I hope you will write me in detail. Otherwise my impatience is not that strong, and I am put to shame by all the love that I have not earned. As I returned to my cell today I found a very fine book there from Dora Langer.[2] Then I ate and took an afternoon nap. The rest of the day I wrote but the mountain is growing constantly bigger in spite of that. We will have to keep the collective-answer system. Holstein was here too, the loyal one! Oh darling, what might God have planned for us?! I am neither ambitious nor revolutionary minded, am neither a theologian nor anything else, and we are being forced to appear before all the world! Here I now stand, a poor fool! So we at least want to stand steadfastly! My heartfelt greetings, beloved, beloved wife!

Always,
Your Martin

1. This day was Niemöller's birthday, and he was inundated by greetings. To express thanks to as many as possible who had sent birthday wishes, Else Niemöller had the following letter duplicated on February 19:

On my husband's birthday he and I received many wishes, evidencing friendship and brotherhood. At my husband's request I would like to thank you from my heart for so much love and faith! It helps him and me to be able to see and experience every day, and especially on a special day like his birthday, how great the group is that stands with us and how many of them pray for us.

My husband is strengthened by seeing from all the letters that he has taken his path in the company of a great Christianity. So please accept, in this sense, thanks from both of us!

2. Dora Langer was a secretary who served the Confessing church through the years.

January 17, 1938
To Mrs. Else Niemöller

My Deloved Else!

It is seven P.M., and an important evening is drawing to a close. Holstein will inform you immediately, as I requested. God help us now, and you, my love, to have strength for another two months! I had just received the books this afternoon (*The Father, We Are Chasing German Submarines, Weyer, The Psalms*) and was conversing with Dr. Koch, whom I had not seen in ten days, when Holstein brought the news.[1] Now another life begins again: files and conferences. The mail will have to take a back seat. I haven't received any more since the last stack of 450 pieces. Today in court I was shown, I think, about 4,000. I will get the important ones and the great bulk of them will be shelved until after the trial. I write you an occasional thanks "to all." Who is the English book *The Psalms* from? And what kind of book did the crew send me? Who sent the pullover? I would like to have everything organized beforehand.

I am expecting you—alone—on Thursday; I have to talk to you about my suit for the trial day! The whole world looks different than it did. But I am very happy even though the continued imprisonment will be difficult! For my birthday an

Editha Vorgang (who is she?) wrote me the quote from Joshua 1:9* and I have it in front of me to my great consolation! I will miss Wehrhahn very much in the coming weeks. It is generally somewhat lonely for me (Vogel is still on his honeymoon trip). My thoughts of you are all the more heartfelt, love. I do not know what the churchmen are planning now. If it is nothing too pressing, it would be best if they waited until after the trial for the big "meeting"?! Please talk to Fritz Müller before you come to me Thursday. I have already written to my parents and to Heinz Hermann. Please tell Brigitte and Wilhelm as well as Niesel and Jacobi! My dear Else, I take you tightly in my arms. May our faithful Lord stand by us and guide his affairs himself! And what we are to bear consequently, let us bear bravely! Greetings to all; a kiss to you!

Your happy
Martin

*"This is my command: be strong, be resolute; do not be fearful or dismayed, for the Lord your God is with you wherever you go."

1. Immediately after a court date for the trial had been set, as Holstein reported, the second provisional directorate of the German Evangelical church (Albertz, Böhm, Forck, Fricke, Müller) ordered the following announcement to be made from the pulpit on January 30: "The trial against Martin Niemöller is to begin before the special court in Berlin on February 7. The congregations will remember him in their faithful prayers. The trial has been expected for a long time. Questions vital to Christianity will be decided in this trial. May God help to make this trial a blessing for our Evangelical church and our German people."

January 19, 1938
To Mrs. Else Niemöller

My Dearest Else!
Your letter of the 13th which I received today among many others, including yours of the 16th, rouses all my sympathy. Can't you do anything at all about getting to bed earlier? You really ought to be asleep by eleven o'clock; then you wouldn't be bothered by the early rising. But just hold on; we're before a new situation now, and I'm sure you'll make it through these next two months too! . . .

I was just interrupted by my mail, which included your card of the 17th. . . . I'm really somewhat confused by all of it, and it's so difficult to get through the many views scattered throughout the letters. Stratenwerth indicates there are new attempts at mediation by Bodelschwingh. And good Zimmermann, Jr.,[1] even thinks we are at the same point as early in 1933 and that the little group is getting even smaller. Fritz Müller writes very kindly, but has nothing to say about the matter, while people who used to be unsure partisans, or even "neutral," now send warm greetings admonishing me to stand fast! Well, I'm doing what I can, and I'm confident that the rightness of the path must follow from the word of God and not from human judgments!

Tomorrow you'll be here, I hope. And afterwards all three lawyers will be with me. I'm of good cheer, and think it out of the question that my court date could be postponed once more. I've just got a cold now and headaches with it; I hope that by tomorrow or the day after it will be over! I think back with great thanks to your birthday visit, and in general I reflect on the lovely peace of these months with a quiet regret. As far as my health and my spirit are concerned, it's really helped more than it has harmed. . . .

I'm really curious to know what old tall G. will say about my trial; Wehrhahn wrote me a *very fine* birthday letter, truly excellent. The man has an irreproachable soul, such as I can only wish for our children. Jessen's faithfulness, and Eisenhardt's too, moves me deeply; such devotion to the cause is a great consolation to me. And all the young people—many, very many students—have written, from Rostock, Göttingen, Erlangen, Tübingen. And the academic youth of Switzerland and England are well represented too. That 500-600 young people were in Dahlem is a joy as well. . . .

Dibelius and his wife wrote again very kindly; even Vits (!) sent a greeting. Among the best was a letter from Knak[2] with the entire mission house! . . . From Basel there was a letter from D. Thurneysen,[3] from England one from George Bell of Chichester[4] with Frey's commentary. It's wonderful! That's the kind of theologian I'd like to be! . . . I've stopped all other reading for lack of time, and tomorrow you'll have another package of books to take away. I must have more room and air! . . .

1. Superintendent Richard Zimmerman, Jr. (b. 1877), of the St. Bartholomew Church in Berlin was a member of the Prussian district church committee.

2. D. Siegfried Knak was director of the Berlin Mission Society from 1921 to 1949.

3. Professor D. Eduard Thurneysen (b. 1888) was a close friend of Karl Barth. He was Professor of Practical Theology in Basel since 1930.

4. George Bell (1883–1958), Lord Bishop of Chichester, became head of the central and executive committee of the World Council of Churches at its founding. He interceded repeatedly for the imprisoned Martin Niemöller through letters to the editor of the *Times,* through special prayer services, and in other ways.

Cf. *George Bell/Alphons Koechlin Briefwechsel, 1933–1954* ed. with an introduction and commentary by Andreas Lindt (Zurich, 1969).

January 20, 1938
To Mrs. Else Niemöller

Beloved Else!
Until just a little while ago (three P.M.) the lawyers were here, and we "worked" a bit. But I haven't acquired a taste for the business yet; it's sure to come "with eating"! And that was a beautiful reunion this morning; Jochen looks very well, and his manner pleased me very much. I was also satisfied with the way Sass looks; at any rate he seemed refreshed! Who is to hold the meeting of the confirmation parents now? Will Dibelius come to it? I ought to have the list soon if I'm to do anything about the sayings; I'd also like to know what groups the children want to be confirmed in (also because of the sayings!) Tomorrow I'll write to Müller; and I'd like to begin really "working" then too.

I was so happy to hear the results of Tini's check-up. God grant that the little one will be quite healthy soon! I'm worried about Wilhelm; perhaps Fritz ought to speak with Sauerbruch about it since the idea of an operation does scare me.

Niesel should write something about the situation of the church; I haven't the least notion of what's going on.[1] I'm not impatient, I just hope we're not marching backward! It's secondary whether the motion forward is faster or slower. Did you get the books all right today? Next week you'll probably have to take away another such load! Say hello to everyone, especially Jan, Hertha, Jutta! For you dearest, a warm kiss; I wish you lots of strength and joy! "Be not sorrowful!"

Your Martin

---

1. Niesel could have reported, for instance, that on January 11 at 9:30 A.M. there was a meeting in the Dahlem parish house of all those concerned with education. At eleven o'clock the meeting was ended by the state police. The participants were all banished from Berlin, while Niesel, who lived in Berlin, was prohibited from leaving the city (which didn't hinder him, however, from doing so on occasion).

January 23, 1938
To Mrs. Else Niemöller

Dearest Else!
. . . My work has thrived in these last days; there is sure to be a rather considerable altercation after all. But I have a very good conscience in all this; it is also nice to be going to the front lines again, as in Proverbs 31:8: "Open your mouth for the dumb, for the rights of all who are left desolate." Only it is a sad sign of the condition which our church has gotten into that these words must be spoken by a pastor of the fields and woods when all winter long we have fed so many bishops, general superintendents, presidents, and consistorial councilmen,[1] all of whom, with the exception of Dibelius,[2] scrambled off the minute the shooting started! John 10. . . .

I'd like to thank the "intercession congregation" for the wonderful Christmas greetings, especially in the hope that a vacation after my trial will give me an opportunity to read Walter's[3] work in peace. I am really grateful, though—not for this gift, but rather for the service that was and still is incomparably more important to me! I have truly felt the outstretched hands that have carried me, praying, through all these months of imprisonment. And I pray to God that he, in his mercy, also hears my prayers for the congregation and that he keeps and preserves us together in true faith! But my prayer is the prayer of the apostle in the last chapter of Ephesians: "Pray on every occasion in the power of the Spirit. To this end keep watch and persevere, always interceding for all God's people; and pray for me, that I may be granted the right words when I open my mouth, and may boldly and freely make known his hidden purpose, for which I am an ambassador—in chains. Pray that I may speak it boldly, as it is my duty to speak."

Those several thousand letters and cards being held till after the trial by the court, as agreed, will have to be sorted first and then—where necessary—answered. I am a bit horrified at the thought of all that; but it must and will work out. . . .

In the meantime it's gotten to be five o'clock; outside the

148

cell doors are rattling: tea and dinner. My day's work is finished; afterwards I'll read a bit in the story of Abraham with Frey's fine commentary. Please buy me any of it that you can get your hands on! I have Second Isaiah (*The Book of God's World Policy*) and Genesis 12–25 (*The Book of Faith*). Surely there must be a Genesis 1–11 (*The Book of Beginnings*). The publisher is Calwer Vereinsbuchhandlung Stuttgart. Have Gustav Warneck send me anything else there is available or is published in the future. . . .

Tomorrow it will be twenty-three years since the battle of Dogger Bank where the *Blücher* was lost. To this day I am still furious when I think about how we waited for the order to sail until it was too late. Now Ingenohl is long since dead;[4] what a shame for the over-exercised fleet and the overly-clever leadership which knew so much and could do so much that they couldn't make a decision. And how similar it was in 1933 with our church and her "leadership." Who was it that said, "The only thing anyone ever learns from history is that no one learns from it"? I've always said it more simply and drastically: "Everyone learns only from the mistakes one makes oneself." And if people only really want to! . . .

1. The complaint about the church leaders is nothing new for Niemöller. On one occasion during Bodelschwingh's term as Reich bishop (May 27 to June 24, 1933), when all the deposed general superintendents were together and did not want to resist, Bodelschwingh's "adjutant"—Niemöller—shouted at them: "You think you are general superintendents . . . you're just bumpkins!" and then walked out of the meeting place.

2. Dibelius was, in fact, the only one to send a letter of protest to state commissioner August Jäger on June 27, 1933: "No state commissar can dismiss me from these essential duties of my office. They remain my duties before God." The author of this letter was Martin Niemöller!

3. Johannes von Walter (b. 1876) was a church historian in Rostock from 1921 to 1940. His *Die Geschichte des Christentums* (*The History of Christianity*) was published in four volumes, 1932–38.

4. Admiral Friedrich von Ingenohl (1857–1933) was chief of the high sea fleet in 1915. In the same year he was succeeded by Admiral Hugo von Pohl (1855–1916).

February 1, 1938
To Mrs. Else Niemöller

Beloved Else!

Today was a busy day; this morning I worked with Vogel, and after lunch I worked alone till five. Later I'll go on. In the meantime, mail: today, I received your card of the 25th and also the one from Saturday morning (the 29th). My complaint was totally unjustified, or did you bring the card of the 25th yourself on the 28th? It did *not* come through the mail. But my pleasure was great. This time there were only twenty-four pieces of mail, which is normal for two days. Niesel and Asmussen both wrote very kindly. Please continue to write as much as before; but your letters could be a bit more detailed!

Please, do not worry! "Worry is the creator's right." My health is fine again today, and I look forward calmly to the trial: the issue is merely the legal judgment of what I am duty bound to say and do as a Christian and a pastor, so really it is only indirectly "my" cause; in actuality it is for the right to preach the gospel to our people.[1] And the same thing holds true now as it did last August: the cause is worth it! And the Confessing church will live; despite all setbacks, Mrs. Fr. need not worry; I do not believe in the victory of the mythos, despite all the efforts of its representatives!

That you have been in Sevenoaks (1920) is really delightful; I'll have to write that to Rev. Taylor. Today I received a moving letter from a Christian businessman in Chicago, which you must read! Give my regards to the faithful Dahlem congregation and to all our friends. These last days of uncertainty, too, will pass, and I'm glad to know that so many hands are folded for my sake. And now, farewell, my dearest. You don't have it very easy "at my side." If I only had you here! But, "Our help. . . ." Say hello to everyone at home, especially the children!

Devoted in love,
Your Martin

1. The result of the long negotiations with the defense attorneys was that they presented the judge with a document containing numerous proposals. It included the question raised later during the trial, which ad-

dressed the "List of the 900"—the names of people in all walks of life who had spontaneously volunteered as witnesses for the trial. This list disappeared, apparently together with all the court files. But the significant events of the trial are clearly reconstructed in the files of attorney Dr. Horst Holstein.

February 6, 1938
To Mrs. Else Niemöller

My Dearest Wife!

If I were outside, I would—let it cost what it may—take a walk with you out there in the early spring sunshine at this hour. And since that's not possible and the afternoon coffee has just woken me roughly from my nap, I'd like at least to write you a letter.

I must begin with my thanks to you for having gotten through to see me once again yesterday. It is dear to me to know that, despite all the knocks of this recent time, you expect nothing other of me than that I fight bravely. The devil hasn't made it easy for me these last days; and the last great block he has rolled into my path—I hope it's the last!—is this business with the exclusion of the public from my trial.[1] I don't know if I don't owe it to Jesus' cause, now that I'm not to defend it publicly, just to remain silent and to release my lawyers! I know it would be foolish, seen humanly, and that I'd then get no judgment at all—or a hard one—and give the judges a clear conscience for their decision. And then I ask myself if, in the end, the public judgment would not be sufficient, since the reasons for the judgment will be made public too. But who can assure me that the important things will be touched on or even hinted at, then? I thought about it and prayed over it a lot last night, but then I fell asleep. And this morning I'm tending toward the view that I should speak and defend myself after all; but it's more a feeling than a conviction: *"apage Satana!"**

In this quarter hour the heavens clouded over again—it's a pity; the sun shone so joyfully from outside! But things must

*"Begone, Satan!"

go on even within the sun of this world! "Go hence, another sun . . . !" I'm surprised that despite everything I'm so cheerful and at peace. My work for tomorrow has been ready since yesterday evening; the papers are set, except for those that a closer look showed me to be missing. If I only had everything the police carted away, I could handle the first two weeks alone! But what's gone is gone, and "let it be gone! The kingdom . . ."

I slept well and peacefully last night; only toward morning before waking I dreamt of a rotating church spire and of a large dog like "Schnauz" which bit Fritz and me alternately. When Fritz rescued me from the dog, it bit him, and when I grabbed its tail to make it let go of Fritz, it got me. Since I don't understand about dreams, the meaning escapes me; but I suppose that it is the back and forth between Tini's gland and his eye that assumes such a peculiar form. And since you see me wearing a halo, as you wrote in your letter of February 1, here is your "St. Martin" fighting the "dragon!" What's left is the rotating church tower, and that may be an image (according to Morgenstern), not for the great Galileo's "but it moves nevertheless!" but for the fact that, despite all the alarming changes, the church of Jesus "stands and will stand." I can tell you this image was more frightening than the biting dog, even though I've been afraid enough of that since the time I was in high school and the Wöstemeyers' watchdog in Alstede near Ibbenbüren leaped at me and knocked his forelegs at my chest so that I thought, "This is it!" But the scare was the worst of it, and "he moves nevertheless!"

This morning I enjoyed my walk in the yard, and afterward the service which was held by Pastor Lemke (Klatt is still absent). We sang hymns 356 and 172, and the sermon was about the end of Matthew 7: the double metaphor of house-building, on sand and on rock. It was very, very good for me! Then I wrote cards to Dora, Grete, Miss Unverdorben, Hermann, Jochen, and my parents, and at lunch Pastor Lemke dropped in to visit. Then I took a nap and read *Huttens Letzte Tage* (*Hutten's Last Days*) by Conrad Ferdinand Meyer. The book came in yesterday's mail from an anonymous sender in Bochum. It must have been Mrs. von Heydebreck again. I had forgotten a lot of it: "I do believe, no harm shall come/to the man for whom a child addresses God." And I had to tell myself again how rich we are, after all, in our "afflictions."

Yesterday afternoon I received "only" 146 pieces of mail—and in the evening I read them *all*! I've had no letters from you for the 29th or the 30th. The last was from the 26th, and now the one of February 1/2. But I am happy to have these; Wilhelm's letter arrived too, to my great delight. Your card of February 3 is here too. I am sorry now that I didn't select the confirmation sayings earlier. Because should the trial come to a negative conclusion, which I must *also* consider a possibility, then these and similar opportunities will cease. I'm returning the sermon by Fritz Müller. I hope you'll be able to take the big package of books on Wednesday; and on the 19th you may have to cart off another! I also had a card from Brigitte in which she wrote of possibly being in Dahlem this week. But I suppose you discussed that with her by phone?! I shall be surprised if I see you tomorrow morning in court. My head is clear, and I'm hoping it will remain so! The lawyers were all somewhat under pressure yesterday; well, they have all sorts of things to worry about. I'm happy I'm no lawyer; despite everything, it is a finer task to deal in the gospel of Jesus than in the laws of Moses. And yet both are needed in this world.

Darling, I wish you much strength! You have become old, and these months won't disappear so quickly from your face. I think you've gotten the heavier load in all this. But I think of you faithfully and in great love, and I pray constantly that our heavenly father may stand by your side. Hello to all the children; their cards invigorated me! Greetings also to our friends; I was so pleased to be able to shake hands with Mrs. F.[2] "Excelsior" says Father Niemöller, and "sursum corda" is written in the liturgy: "Our help stands in the name of the Lord!" With love and fidelity.

Always,
Your Martin

Tell Käthe Dilthey my thanks for her message, same to the Niesels!

1. On February 4 the state attorneys applied for the exclusion of the public from the trial.
2. Mrs. F. could be Mrs. Elsa Freudenberg.

PART V
February 7, 1938
through
March 1, 1938

These final letters were written during the trial which began on February 7 and concluded, after a ten-day recess, on February 26. During the course of the trial, Niemöller is persuaded to reappoint his attorneys, and we find not only them actively engaged in his defense (see the letter of February 14) but also Niemöller himself making a final statement on the closing day of the trial (see the note to the letter of February 24).

Niemöller's reference to "Symanowsky" (sic) in the letter of February 14 is an intriguing one, and the footnote unfortunately provides only the briefest of detail. In *The Nazi Persecution of the Churches: 1933 – 1945* (New York: Basic Books, 1969), John Conway identifies Czymanowski as the Protestant pastor Ernst Biberstein who was appointed to his first parish in 1924, became a member of the Nazi party in 1927, was appointed to the Reich ministry of church affairs in 1935, and became a member of the S.S. in 1936. After serving in Holland and France as a corporal in the Wehrmacht, he was transferred in 1940 to serve under Reinhard Heydrich—Himmler's assistant and chief of the security police (1936 – 42)—as chief of security police in Oppeln (Silesia). Biberstein later became leader of the notorious Einsatzkommando Unit 6 (the death squad units) in southern Russia. He was condemned to death in the Nuremberg trials of 1947, but four years later his sentence was commuted and he was released.

Of the trial itself, one Nazi official is said to have observed, "This trial is one of the most shameful and unworthy spectacles I have everwitnessed. . . . No reliable evidence has been forthcoming. . . . Such trials should not and must not be allowed to take place in Germany."

As for Niemöller himself, on the final day of the trial he was finally able to make the defense that, for him, was the real issue at stake. As his biographer recounts,

> Speaking quietly, without trace of heat, he said that the trial sprang from the cleavage which had arisen between the new ideology and the teaching of the church and from the attempt to impose the one upon the other. Once again he expressed his belief that limits were set to human authority, including that of the totalitarian state; those limits were the gospel of Jesus Christ.
>
> "The state, mankind, the whole world," he said in conclusion, "will rob themselves of their true destiny and their ultimate goal if they fail to respect or recognize the frontier here drawn."

Dietmar Schmidt, *Pastor Niemöller*
(ET New York: Doubleday, 1959)

February 7, 1938
To Mrs. Else Niemöller

My Little Else!

The day was hard, but I survived it well;[1] neither my head nor stomach are giving me trouble, and I'm enjoying the last hour before retiring with one of my "black girl friends." I find speaking somewhat difficult after the long pause; I keep tripping over my own tongue. But I think that should improve from day to day. And my inner peace is greater even than it used to be at critical moments in wartime, where I was well known for my calmness! I also have to get accustomed to the rapidity of the proceedings, but I'm sure I shall! In any case I look back on this first day with thanks to God.

Toward day's end I also received lots of mail, including your painfully missed letter of the 29th. But the time flies; I've always got some work to do in between, too, to keep my memory caught up! The letter from Mrs. Volkenborn is moving; it made me so happy to know I have such a brave and well-loved wife. Today I saw you only at a distance, but it was lovely anyway. Who was the nice lady (who looked like Mrs. Curtius or Mrs. Jessen) with the pretty young girl? I was really pleased to see some dear faces again, even from afar! The lawyers are apparently satisfied with me. I hope the court will be too, in the end! The most important day for me will be tomorrow. So dear, say hello from me to the children, Müller, Asmussen, Sass (whom I also saw), and Eisenhardt. Good old Albertz was there with his wife. I also saw Rabender and Jacobi—Diestel was there too; there's something fatherly and calming about him, probably due to the big white beard. I am confident that I will hold up well, God grant! For Thursday we have the beautiful selection from 2 Chronicles 32, "We have the Lord our God to help us and to fight our battles" (from my lecture "Die belagerte Gottesstadt" ["The Beleagured City of God"]. Now good night, more tomorrow.

Devotedly and truly,
Your Martin

1. February 7 was the first day of the trial. Many who had waited since the previous evening in front of the courthouse were turned away on that day. At first only the closest relatives of the defendant were granted entry. An ecumenical representative, the dean of Chichester, Dr. Duncan Jones, was excluded, as were representatives of the Confessing church. Superintendent Max Diestel was allowed into room 664 because he was the defendant's legal superior. Otherwise, only members of the state and police authorities were present. The instructions to the press put out by the propaganda ministry included the sentence: "The trial is not to be mentioned at all."

In the meantime, the judges were reappointed. The presiding judge was Dr. Robert Hoepke, the attending judges Dr. Welz and Hans Schwarz.

February 8, 1938
To Mrs. Else Niemöller

My Dearest Else!

So I did what I had written you; there was no other choice.[1] Thus, "everything is lost, but not my honor." My last consultation with my lawyers will belong to my most beautiful memories till my end; we were able to conclude it with a prayer that I spoke! So now I'm entirely in the passive, in suffering, and yet am aware that this is not weakness, but rather strength, not resignation, but rather action! The trial is now adjourned till the 19th, and I expect that is not the "last word." But we must remember that God guides our path, and his doing is always love! This too must serve for the "advancement of the gospel," surely; and it will now be our and the congregation's lesson assigned us by the savior: Matthew 5:44.*

It is reassuring to me that I will see you tomorrow; for my heart trembles at the thought that your strength may give out! But you know the source from which we may and should draw; and the Christian community will carry and support us with its prayer all the more now. Give my greetings to the congregation and tell them that I place my entire confidence in God's mercy, and that I am convinced that one day we will recognize in the light the paths along which he leads us now in the darkness and that we will praise his wisdom! God does not desire to give us earthly hopes, but he will certainly not abandon us. Jesus Christ remains the same, that is certain; and God will grant us that "we remain with him!" "Our path leads to the stars,/it is planted with crosses./Here we need not depart/although it be covered with blood./Those who live inside Salem's walls/show their crowns of thorns." Dearest Else, in him we are close together and with him we are well protected! In him and with him our children shall remain, that is my prayer today! Say hello to everyone, especially my parents, Wilhelm, the children, and those at home. "He is worthy that we honor him and expend ourselves in his service."

Devotedly,
Your Martin

*"But what I tell you is this: Love your enemies and pray for your persecutors."

1. On this second day of the trial, Niemöller, helplessly exposed to the constant insults of the district attorney who spoke of treasonous contact with foreign countries, declared he would no longer tolerate such attacks: "I will no longer testify, and I release my lawyers."

The proceedings are reported in depth by Wilhelm Niemöller, *Macht geht vor Recht: Der Prozess Martin Niemöllers* (Munich, 1952).

February 9, 1938
To Pastor Wilhelm Niemöller

My Dear Wilhelm!
Your greeting of the 6th brought me great pleasure, and now God grant that you continue to improve! I stand again before a door slammed shut: waiting and patient. So today's reading selection was especially applicable to me. *Providentia specialissima*! Good, that standing on *this* ground we can cheerfully speak our "nevertheless," "You hold me in your right hand!" Now things go as per 2 Timothy 4:17a* and Ephesians 3:13.** Hello to all your loved ones, especially Wilhelm, whom I thank warmly for his letter.

Sincerely,
Your devoted Martin

*"But the Lord stood by me and lent me strength, so that I might be his instrument in making the full proclamation of the Gospel for the whole pagan world to hear."
**"I beg you, then, not to lose heart over my sufferings for you; indeed, they are your glory."

February 10, 1938
To Unknown

... I am physically and spiritually well; what is to become of me is in God's hand and does not cause me concern any longer, and I do not worry about it anymore either. For us the path is clear: "Preach the word, hold fast, be it the right time or the wrong time!" God has granted that we flourish and thrive. We pray that he will continue to do so. The gospel is not defense, but rather attack, and it is up to the world to decide its position! The gospel is glad tidings; and we will not allow the gladness it gives to be taken from us! Let us go forward!

February 14, 1938
To Mrs. Else Niemöller

Dearest Wife!
Now it's been a week since the opening day of my trial; strange—it seems to me an eternity—although the intervening days simply flew by. I count 229 days since my arrest, and yet I see July 1 before my mind's eye as if it were yesterday. "I am not a perfected book, I am a man with all his contradictions." Outside it's winter again, but the kind one has to enjoy: with snow and luminous sun, so that even my cell is extraordinarily bright. Our lilac trees outside have already grown fat buds, but now they'll have to acknowledge their error and wait a while longer. They are a bit like us in their impatience. Nevertheless, winter is half over, the days are noticeably longer, and on March 21 spring begins!
Today is a quiet day; the lawyers haven't shown up yet, and the mail apparently needs a running start to overcome its Sunday rest. This morning I cleaned my window, which the sun seems to honor in a friendly fashion; and then I wrote a number of cards which will wander out to north, south, east, and west tomorrow! My thoughts are constantly on the road in the scattered congregation. . . .

Now it's three o'clock in the afternoon; will surprises never cease? Not only did they serve boiled beef instead of roast; but it was actually the "three faithful ones"* who called me, and I was able to give them a new power of attorney. Now the trial is to continue *Friday*. I shan't be surprised if we get over the stuttering finally. The three claim to have had more to do in these last days than with the entire trial so far. For my part, I cannot claim any such thing. . . .

I have not been depressed, that is not my inclination. If you were to write me the churches are empty, the temporary leadership is being dissolved, the bishops are making their peace with Symanowsky[1]—well, then, I'd probably not be too pleased. But currently, I have no reason to be pessimistic— the church's line since 1933 is a straight one, and what more do we want? . . .

---

*A reference to his three attorneys. On the second day of the trial, Niemöller had decided no longer to speak in his own defense and had released his attorneys (see footnote to letter of February 8).

1. "Czymanowski" was provost in Segeburg, district head of Magdeburg-Anhalt (a church district created by the Nazis), and a collaborator of the Reich ministry of church affairs.

February 19/20, 1938
To Mrs. Else Niemöller

My Dear, Dear Else!
I had *no* headache today, was fresh and able to concentrate well on business. The lawyers were satisfied, and so was I. You know that I can't and don't want to make a murderer's den out of my heart. The cause is too good and I see myself as above taking advantage of a "right" as it is granted a "defendant." . . . So it may be that here and there the lawyers would have me be somewhat more "cautious." But: "Were I prudent, my name wouldn't be Tell."

By the way, my mental powers are beginning to be released again from their bound condition of "potential energy." It is a peculiar sensation for me, as if something were beginning to flow that had been blocked for a long time. And this is probably, and maybe primarily, the reason I am now feeling better than at any other time in these eight months; it's a kind of increased vitality that I must think and speak in a responsible fashion. And this "standing in the decision" may well be the actual process that makes life worth living. The "stuttering" or the *feeling* of stuttering is past, and my cell is no longer narrow! And in all this, strangely enough, the thought of how it shall end plays as little a role as it did during the war in the middle of a depth-charge attack. The moment is everything, time and eternity in one. Of course, outside the courtroom I don't feel in the least like looking at the files. I don't know how to explain it; it is not mere surfeit or laziness, but surely includes the unconscious knowledge that the decisions are being made in solitude on entirely different points.

But I don't want to bore you with psychology; besides, it's supposed to be a sign of old age when one starts studying one's own psyche in the mirror. But perhaps all this will calm you somewhat in your thoughts of your husband! Last night I slept beautifully from 10:30 to 5:30. I dreamt of consistorial councillor Görs, with the result that he appeared in the courtroom today representing the consistory! Isn't that funny? The lawyers were fine; Holstein takes care of me like a governess to make sure nothing is forgotten. It's probably just as well; I am amazed now at the carefree fashion with which I went into this business of the trial, the laws and mechanics of which I hadn't the vaguest notion. I think it's downright amusing to the others; and I wonder if I don't cut as seriocomic a figure as old Bodelschwingh did in the Reichstag. But what shall I do? Now I'm in it and must get through with inner dignity; it's just that I notice I'm quite ignorant of the finesses; but there's a reason for the saying, "The dear Lord protects the children and the drunks" (I'm counting myself in the first category of course).

Tomorrow is the day of rest, a Sunday *with* services, and I look forward to it sincerely. The hectic rush that I have behind me I don't want ever to start on again; and I don't believe that God asks it of me. Well, we'll see! In any case, I want to enjoy the lovely book by Chambon tomorrow. Holstein mentioned something today which of course went in one ear and out the other, that you were invited to their place tomorrow (?) or one of the next evenings. We should be grateful for all these small favors which God grants us in our "affliction"! And yesterday you were—with Brigitte!—at the Kochs, and Hahn told me you had driven him home in P.'s car! After yesterday's "poetic" outpouring about Wednesday's events, I received Jan's "The Course of a Day." What a joy. Oh, dear, I do love to laugh. And such products of the German spirit are really "balm for a broken heart." Today someone reminded me in a card that I had once spoken of "God's humor"; that "humor" belongs, for me, to the archetypal image of the "father"; and that Father Niemöller has this humor, has been a special note for my life since earliest childhood. . . .

Müller and Niesel both wrote quite optimistically about the development of the church and the congregation, but pessimistically about the attitude of the bishops. That doesn't cause me too much concern, because I have always been and still am convinced that the decision will fall in Prussia. And in this Asmussen is perfectly correct in his demand that the church's efforts consciously choose the individual parish for its target. These must be *intensive* efforts, through and through, as the course of the last five years has shown. . . .

A piece of news I must report is that Krenzlin[1] wrote to me! I really hadn't thought it possible, but it was a pleasure. And the farmer Beiderwellen[2] (if I'm not mistaken, a childhood friend of Paul Herring) wrote a very sweet letter from Wersen. I really must go back home again, and in case I'm released from prison, I'd prefer that to the idea of a holiday in the Riesen mountains. You must remember the old quotation from the days of Professor D. Heim in Münster: "I only want Heim."[*] They say Otto Schitz coined it. The Westphalian pastors sent a greeting in cumulo through superintendent Niederstein[3] from the conference in Dortmund. Even a year ago that wouldn't have been possible; in those days these Christians were still divided under Zoellner's outdated slogans! A sign that during these eight months time has not stood still after all. The coming days will not be quite so fatiguing for me personally as the last ones were. But I don't give thoughts of the trial too much room, but am just happy that it's to go on tomorrow. . . .

[*] A pun on the speaker's name and "I only want to go home."

1. Paul Krenzlin was the president of the state office for cultural affairs in Berlin; he played a significant role in the life of the church, especially in his capacity as an expert in questions of law. He died at the age of ninety-five.

2. Wilhelm Beiderwellen (b. 1884) was a farmer and church master in Wersen, and later a representative at the Westphalian district synod.

3. Superintendent Alfred Niederstein (b. 1866) was a pastor in Altenbochum and superintendent of the Bochum county synod and also chairman of the Westphalian pastor's association for many decades. The Westphalian pastor's association supported the cause of the Confessing church like none other in Germany, as evidenced by the incomparably higher number of its members in the Confessing church.

February 24, 1938
To Mrs. Else Niemöller

Dear Little Else!

Pity, that you were late at noon today; I would have liked to have taken the sight of you with me. This was the most difficult of these 239 days. But after lunch I worked a while with the lawyers, and now I still have quite a bit to do. So you must forgive me for writing only this card. You do not need to worry; I'm really very well, and I know that I'm no criminal; I will sleep well tonight and return to my work tomorrow.[1] I am a bit concerned about the days of waiting—Saturday, Sunday, Monday? Tuesday? Wednesday? I don't know yet. The Bible calls God the "God of patience and of solace." That means *me* with the "patience" and *you* with the "solace"!

It was good that my only mail today was your letter; say hello to Brigitte especially, and God help you all that you may be not a burden, but a help, to each other! It may yet be very necessary. My strength is nearly at an end too, but it must and will suffice for these next days. And I will not think now of what may come afterward. If we are to suffer, then there too, and especially there, the Lord Jesus will make known his strength and glory to us! Please call my parents and give them my special love, and tell them I'm thinking a lot of mother's cold. Then say hello also to Müller, Niesel, Asmussen. I hope they will be with you in these days! And now goodbye for today, my dear heart; may God grant you his solace daily and plentifully, as he may grant me the strength and patience! Give all the children a kiss; my only wish to all of them is that they may carry and support you as best they can!

Devotedly and faithfully in love,
Your Martin

1. On February 25, 1938, the session began at 9:40 A.M. with Dr. Holstein's speech for the defense and continued later with the speeches of Dr. Koch and Dr. Hahn.
    On February 26 the session began at 9:10 A.M. The prosecution and the defense came to words over the notices in the foreign press. The defendant's final words followed, and the session concluded at 12:45.

March 1, 1938
To Pastor Wilhelm Niemöller

My Dear and Faithful Brother!
Today I received your card of the 25th with great pleasure. The days of waiting are nearing their end, and tomorrow at noon the judgment will be spoken. Everything else is uncertain, but I am happy and hopeful, whatever the judgment and whatever may happen to me afterward.[1] But let me give you my heartfelt love once more; it is good that I have you as my brother and that I know that in any case someone will take care of my loved ones! "The Lord is my helper!" My love to your family.

Warmly,
Your Martin

1. The verdict and sentence—which would have left Niemöller a free man—was rendered on March 2, 1938. That same evening Martin Niemöller was in the concentration camp in Sachsenhausen as prisoner No. 569.

INDEX